Les Misérables

Adaptation and activities by **Gina D. B. Clemen**

Illustrated by **Paolo Rui**

Series editor: Robert Hill
Editor: Maria Grazia Donati
Design and art direction: Nadia Maestri
Computer graphics: Carlo Cibrario-Sent, Simona Corniola
Picture research: Alice Graziotin

© 2016 Black Cat

First edition: January 2016

Picture credits :
Shutterstock; Istockphoto; Dreamstime; Thinkstock; DeAgostini Picture
Library: 4, 52, 53, 54, 102, 119; Getty Images: 5h, 81; © George Brice/Alamy
Stock Photo: 18; Bibliotheque des Arts Decoratifs, Paris, France/Bridgeman
Images: 19; The Print Collector/Print Collector/Getty Images: 55;
adoc-photos/Contrasto: 64; © Leemage/Corbis: 77; Sylvain Grandadam/
Marka: 78; Marka: 80; © Brian Seed/Bridgeman Images: 103; © VIDEA/
WebPhoto: 104; WebPhoto: 105; IFPA/Marka: 106; © Universal Pictures/
Courtesy Everett Collection/Contrasto: 120h; © UNIVERSAL PICTURES/
WebPhoto: b, 121; STAN HONDA/AFP/Getty Images: 122h; © Michael
Le Poer Trench/Sygma/Corbis: b; © Stephen Chung/Alamy Stock Photo:
123h; Dave Benett/Getty Images: ch; Mark Sullivan/WireImage/Getty
Images: cb; Phil Robinson/Marka: b.

Contents

Chapters 1, 2, 3, 4, 5, 6, 7, 8 are recorded on the accompanying CD.

Chapter 9 is downloadable from our website: blackcat-cideb.com

These symbols indicate the beginning and end of the passages

linked to the listening activities.

 blackcat-cideb.com

About the author

Victor Hugo was born in Besançon, France, on 26 February 1802. He was an excellent student and started writing poems when he was still very young. In July 1816, at the age of fourteen, he wrote this sentence in a notebook: 'I want to be Chateaubriand or nothing.' François-René de Chateaubriand was a famous French writer during the early 19th century, who was considered the founder of Romanticism [1] in French literature.

1. **Romanticism** : in the early 19th century many writers and artists believed in the importance of individual feelings, the power of freedom and the beauty of language and dreams.

Victor Hugo statue in Guernsey, Channel Islands.

Victor Hugo studied law between 1815 and 1818, but he never worked as a lawyer. He wanted to become a great writer. He founded the *Conservateur littéraire*, a journal in which he published his own poetry and the work of his friends.

In 1831 he published his great novel, *Notre-Dame de Paris* (known in English as *The Hunchback of Notre-Dame*). Hugo became an important writer in France in the 1840s, and was elected to the prestigious [2] French Academy. During his life he was deeply concerned with social injustice, poverty and political problems of his times.

His masterpiece, *Les Misérables*, was published in 1862, and it was an immediate success in Europe and the United States. *Les Misérables* is one of the best-known works of 19th century literature, and it has inspired theatrical plays, musicals and films. In this book Victor Hugo describes and criticises the social injustice in France between the fall of Napoleon in 1815 and the failed revolution against King Louis-Philippe in 1832.

2. **prestigious** : very important and significant.

The title *Les Misérables* is a French phrase that cannot be translated exactly into English. In French it has two meanings. It means 'people who live in misery'; [3] and it also means, 'people who live outside society in total poverty'.

Upton Sinclair, one of America's great writers, described *Les Misérables* as 'one of the half-dozen greatest novels of the world.'

Hugo became one of the most important and respected French writers. During his life he wrote twenty books of poetry, nine novels and ten plays, and a huge amount of political writing. On the occasion of his 80th birthday in 1882, the street on which he lived was renamed Avenue Victor Hugo. He died in Paris on 22 May 1885. He received a hero's funeral and was buried in the Panthéon in Paris, where many famous French people are buried.

Comprehension check

1 Answer the following questions.

1 Who was Chateaubriand and how did he affect Victor Hugo's youth?
2 What was the *Conservateur littéraire*?
3 What were Victor Hugo's concerns?
4 What does Victor Hugo describe in *Les Misérables*?
5 What has *Les Misérables* inspired?
6 What happened on Victor Hugo's 80th birthday?
7 What was his funeral like and where was he buried?

Discussion

2 Discuss these questions with a partner.

1 Who were the important writers of the 1800s in your country?
2 Name some of their works.

3. **misery** : sadness, suffering, despair.

Before you read

1 **PRELIMINARY** Listening

Listen to Chapter One and choose the correct answer — A, B, and C.

1 When did the stranger arrive in the town of Digne?
- **A** ☐ in October 1805
- **B** ☐ in October 1850
- **C** ☐ in October 1815

2 Where did the stranger keep his money?
- **A** ☐ in an old leather purse
- **B** ☐ in a heavy soldier's bag
- **C** ☐ in his pocket

3 Who told the stranger about the bishop's home?
- **A** ☐ the innkeeper
- **B** ☐ an old woman
- **C** ☐ the townspeople

4 How many times did Jean Valjean try to escape from prison?
- **A** ☐ fourteen times
- **B** ☐ five times
- **C** ☐ four times

5 Who noticed that the silver was stolen?
- **A** ☐ the bishop
- **B** ☐ the servant
- **C** ☐ the three policemen

2 Reading pictures

Look at the picture on page 15 and answer the following questions.

1 Where are the police taking Jean Valjean?

2 Why are they taking him there?

3 How does Jean Valjean feel at this moment?

The Characters

At the beginning of the story...
From left to right: Jean Valjean, the Bishop of Digne, Mrs Magloire, Fantine, Mr Madeleine, Inspector Javert, Mr Thénardier, Mrs Thénardier, young Cosette, young Éponine, young Azelma.

Some years later...
From left to right: Fauchelevent, Cosette, Mrs Thénardier, Mr Thènardier Éponine, Azelma, Marius Pontmercy, Mr Gillenormand, Gavroche.

Jean Valjean

One evening in October 1815, a man with a long beard and torn clothes walked into the town of Digne. He was in his late forties, of medium height and had a strong body. His face was tired and sunburnt, and he carried a large wooden stick. A heavy soldier's bag was on his back.

The townspeople, who had never seen him before, watched him with interest as he stopped at the fountain for some water. He then crossed the square and walked into an inn.

'What can I do for you, sir?' asked the innkeeper without looking at him.

'A meal and a bed,' said the stranger.

'Of course,' said the innkeeper, who turned and looked at him. The innkeeper saw his rough appearance and added, 'If you can pay for it.'

'I have money,' the stranger showed him an old leather purse.

'Show me your passport,' said the innkeeper.

The stranger took a yellow passport out of his pocket. As soon as the innkeeper saw the yellow passport, which was only given to ex-convicts, he exclaimed 'You can't stay here! You've just come out of prison. I don't want people like you here!'

The stranger got up, took his bag and stick and left. It was getting dark and a cold wind was blowing from the east. He lay down on a stone bench near a church.

A few minutes later an old woman come out of the church and saw him. 'What are you doing?' she asked.

'I need a place to sleep,' said the stranger nervously.

'Go and knock on the door of the bishop's [1] home,' said the old woman, pointing to a door near the church. 'He can help you.'

The Bishop of Digne was a kind old man who had given his palace to the town hospital. He lived a simple life and was loved by the people of the town. His doors were never locked so that anyone who needed his help could find him easily.

The stranger got up from the stone bench and went to knock on the bishop's door.

'Come in,' said the bishop.

The stranger walked in and the bishop looked at his unexpected visitor kindly.

'My name is Jean Valjean,' said the stranger before the bishop could speak. 'I've been in prison for nineteen years and they let

---

1.   **bishop** : an important religious person in the Christian church.

me out four days ago. I've been walking all day and nobody in this town will give me food or a place to sleep. A woman told me to come here. I've got money. Will you let me stay?'

The bishop looked at Mrs Magloire, the old servant, and said, 'Please prepare another place at the table for this gentleman.'

Jean Valjean was surprised and said, 'Perhaps you don't understand. I've spent five years in prison at the Bagne of Toulon for robbery and another fourteen years for trying to escape four times. I'm a dangerous man!'

'Mrs Magloire,' said the bishop calmly, 'please put clean sheets on the bed in the spare room.'

Mrs Magloire, who was an obedient servant, left the room without saying a word.

The bishop looked at the man and said, 'Sit down and warm yourself by the fire. Dinner will soon be ready.'

Jean Valjean's face, which had been angry, suddenly softened. 'You'll let me stay?' he asked, his voice trembling. 'I can pay you.'

'Of course you can stay,' replied the bishop, 'and you can keep your money.'

During dinner the bishop talked about the town's cheese-making industry, but Valjean was so hungry that he paid no attention to anyone at first. Then he began to relax and looked around the room. He noticed the beautiful silver: the candlesticks,[2] knives and forks.

The bishop showed his guest the spare room and said, 'Sleep well, and tomorrow morning you must have a bowl of warm milk from our cows.'

2.   **candlestick** :

Valjean was exhausted and fell asleep immediately, but he didn't sleep for long. He woke up during the night and started thinking about the past twenty years. Life had been unjust to him and he was angry. In 1795 he had lost his job as a tree-cutter. At that time he was looking after his sister, whose husband had died, and her seven children. Out of work and with no food in the house, he had been arrested for trying to steal some bread. Life in prison had been terrible. Now he was finally free, but he felt bitter and angry about his lost years. He wanted revenge.[3] Suddenly he remembered the silver on the bishop's table.

He got up from bed; everything was silent in the bishop's house. He put his shoes into his bag and slowly and quietly went downstairs to the kitchen. He took the silver knives and forks, put them inside his bag and left the bishop's house.

The next morning the servant noticed that the silver was missing and cried, 'Oh no! The silver is gone! The man who came here last night has run off with our silver!'

The bishop looked at his servant and said gently, 'I think I was wrong to keep the silver for so long. It really belongs to the poor. Why didn't I give it away a long time ago?'

Later that morning, while the bishop was having breakfast, someone knocked at the door. Three policemen entered the room with Jean Valjean.

The bishop looked at the three men and smiled at Jean Valjean. 'I'm very pleased to see you again, my dear friend,' he said. 'What about the candlesticks? I gave them to you as well, don't you remember? They're silver like the rest and are probably worth at least two hundred francs. Did you forget to take them?'

---

3. **revenge** : when you want to hurt or punish someone who has hurt you.

CHAPTER ONE

Jean Valjean stared at the bishop; he couldn't believe his ears.

'Was this man telling us the truth?' asked one of the policemen, looking at the bishop.

'Of course he was telling you the truth,' said bishop smiling.

'Well, then this man isn't a thief,' said one of the policemen, looking at the other two.

'Exactly,' said the bishop, 'so you can let him go at once.'

Valjean did not know what to think; he simply stood there.

'Why is this man helping me,' he asked himself. 'What does he want?'

When the three policemen had left, the bishop went to Valjean and said in a low voice, 'Don't forget that you've promised to use the money to make yourself an honest man.'

Valjean, who had never made such a promise, was silent. He looked at the bishop in amazement.

'Jean Valjean,' the bishop continued, 'I've bought your soul from the Devil [4] and I have given it to God.'

Jean Valjean left the town of Digne that morning and went into the countryside. He didn't know where he was going. He kept on walking and walking for hours.

He was confused and filled with a strange kind of anger; he had never felt this way before. During his long stay at the Bagne of Toulon he had been treated horribly by everyone he met. And now for the first time in twenty years a man had shown him great kindness and he didn't know what to feel.

4. **Devil :**

The text and **beyond**

1 PRELIMINARY **Comprehension check**

For questions 1-5, choose the correct answer — A, B, C or D.

1 What did the stranger do before going to the inn?

A ☐ He went to buy a soldier's bag.

B ☐ He picked up a big wooden stick.

C ☐ He went to get some water at the fountain.

D ☐ He stopped to talk to the townspeople.

2 Why didn't the stranger find a place to sleep?

A ☐ because there were no free rooms at the inn

B ☐ because the innkeeper saw his yellow passport

C ☐ because the inn was closed

D ☐ because the stranger didn't have enough money to pay for a room

3 How long did Jean Valjean spend in prison?

A ☐ nineteen years

B ☐ five years

C ☐ fourteen years

D ☐ four years

4 What happened during the night at the bishop's home?

A ☐ Jean Valjean slept for a long time because he was very tired.

B ☐ Jean Valjean left the bishop's home because he couldn't sleep.

C ☐ Jean Valjean stole the bishop's silver candlesticks.

D ☐ Jean Valjean stole the bishop's silver knives and forks.

5 The bishop told the police

A ☐ that he had given Jean Valjean the silver.

B ☐ that he had sold the silver to Jean Valjean.

C ☐ that Mrs Magloire had given Jean Valjean the silver.

D ☐ that Jean Valjean was a dangerous thief.

2 **PRELIMINARY** Sentence transformation
For each question complete the second sentence so that it means the
same as the first. Use no more than three words. There is an example
at the beginning.

0 It was a long journey to Digne.
The journey to Digne ....took.......... a long time.

1 Jean Valjean knocked at the door, but got no answer.
Jean Valjean knocked at the door but .... answered.

2 It's a secret so I can't tell you.
I can't tell you .... it's a secret.

3 The bishop has told you everything.
There is .... the bishop has not told you.

4 There was no one at the inn except the innkeeper.
The innkeeper was .... at the inn.

5 Jean Valjean was younger than Mrs Magloire.
Jean Valjean was not .... Mrs Magloire.

6 There were not many people in the town square.
There were .... people in the town square.

7 Everyone liked the old bishop of Digne.
The old bishop of Digne ....

3 Prediction: what do you think?
Work with a partner and answer these questions. Then compare your
answers with the class.

1 Where will Jean Valjean go now?
2 What will he do?
3 Will he remember the bishop's words and become an honest man?

The Bagne of Toulon

The Bagne of Toulon was a terrible prison in the seaport of Toulon, in the south of France, on the Mediterranean Sea. The *Bagne* was opened in 1748 and it was closed in 1873. During the early 1800s there were about 4,300 prisoners at the Bagne.

King Louis XV created the *bagne* in 1748 for the convicts who had previously been sentenced to row the galleys [1]

The preserved gate of the ancient prison in Toulon which was demolished in 2010.

of the French Mediterranean fleet. The name '*bagne*' came from the Italian word bagno, or bath, the name of a prison in Rome which had once been a Roman bath.

Since the 15th century, French prisoners were sentenced to serve on the galleys where they rowed long hours in horrible conditions. Some of these prisoners were only guilty of stealing some bread because they were hungry!

By the beginning of the 1800s rowing on the galleys had become obsolete, [2] so the prisoners were first moved to a group of ships that were tied up at the port of Toulon, which became floating prisons. Then new prisons were built near the port of Toulon.

1. **galley :**   2. **obsolete :** no longer used, out of date.

A convict in the Toulon Penal Colony,
engraved by De Moraine, c. 1845.

Although the prisoners did not row in the galleys any more, they continued to be sent to Toulon. The convicts were used for digging earth and for construction work. They also worked for big factories near the port. They usually did very dangerous jobs and worked long hours. Sunday was their only free day.

The diet of the prisoners consisted of bread, beans, dried vegetables and a small piece of cold meat and wine for those who had worked during the day. These men did not have real beds – they slept on uncomfortable wooden boards without blankets.

The prisoners wore a special uniform which consisted of a white shirt, yellow trousers, a red vest and a cap. Those who wore green caps were sentenced to life imprisonment, and all the others wore red caps. They had to wear a ring of iron attached to a short chain on their right foot, and the worst convicts were chained together. The chains often weighed between seven and eight kilos.

1 Comprehension check

Answer the following questions.

1   Where was the Bagne of Toulon located?
2   Who created the Bagne of Toulon?
3   Who was sent to the Bagne?
4   What did the prisoners on the galleys do all day long?
5   Why were new prisons built near the port of Toulon?
6   What kind of work did the convicts do?
7   Describe their living conditions.
8   What did the colour of their cap mean?

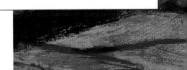

Before you read

1 PRELIMINARY Listening

Listen to Chapter Two and choose the correct answer.

1 The red-haired woman in the village of Montfermeil
  A ☐ was playing with her children.
  B ☐ had two little girls.
  C ☐ was working in the garden of the inn.

2 Fantine told Mrs Thénardier
  A ☐ that her husband was dead.
  B ☐ that she wanted to work at the inn.
  C ☐ that she was going to Paris to meet her husband.

3 Mr Thénardier
  A ☐ did not want to look after Cosette.
  B ☐ wanted money to look after Cosette.
  C ☐ offered Fantine a job at the inn.

4 When Fantine left the village of Montfermeil,
  A ☐ she was happy because she was going to Paris.
  B ☐ she was crying bitterly.
  C ☐ she took a horse and carriage.

5 Fantine went to Montreuil
  A ☐ but did not find any kind of work.
  B ☐ and found a job in a factory.
  C ☐ and became friends with the mayor of the town.

2 Reading pictures

Look at the picture on page 23 and answer the following questions.

1 How many women and children do you see in the picture?
2 What are they doing?
3 Describe the building in the picture.
4 What season of the year is it?

Fantine

I n the spring of 1818, in the village of Montfermeil, near Paris, two little girls were playing outside a small inn. Their mother, a big, red-haired woman with a plain face, sat outside the inn watching them.

'What pretty children you have!' a voice nearby said.

The red-haired woman looked round and saw a young woman with a child sleeping in her arms. The mother was young and pretty, but she looked poor and unhappy. Her thin, pale face was sad, and her clothes were old and dirty. She wore a tight cap over her beautiful blonde hair.

'Thank you,' said the woman. 'Why don't you sit down for a minute? You look rather tired.' The young woman sat down and the red-haired woman introduced herself. 'My name's Thénardier.

CHAPTER **TWO**

My husband and I manage this inn.'

'My name's Fantine,' said the young woman. 'I used to work in Paris but my husband died and I lost my job.'

Fantine could not tell Mrs Thénardier the truth, which was that a young man had made her pregnant and then abandoned her.

Fantine continued her story. 'I left Paris this morning with my little girl because I want to find work in Montreuil.'

Suddenly her daughter woke up and opened her beautiful blue eyes, which looked just like her mother's. She ran to play with the other two girls.

'What's your daughter's name?' asked Mrs Thénardier, looking at the little girl.

'Euphrasie, but I call her Cosette. She's almost three.'

As the children played together, Mrs Thénardier smiled and said, 'Children make friends easily, don't they? They could easily be three sisters.'

When Fantine heard these words she took Mrs Thénardier's hand and said, 'Can you look after my daughter for me?'

Mrs Thénardier was quite surprised but didn't say anything.

'I have to find work, and that's not easy with a child and no husband,' said Fantine. 'As soon as I find a job, I'll come back and get her. Will you do this for me? I can pay you.'

'Of course you must pay us,' said Mr Thénardier, as he came out of the inn. 'Otherwise we cannot look after your daughter. Does she have enough clothes?'

'Oh, yes,' replied Fantine, 'she has lovely silk dresses from Paris.'

Once they had agreed on the amount of money, Fantine kissed her daughter goodbye and left for Montreuil, crying bitterly.

CHAPTER **TWO**

'This money will help me pay my debts and stay out of prison,' thought Mr Thénardier, a cold, cruel man, who always needed money.

The Thénardiers soon sold all of Cosette's silk dresses and dressed her in rags.[1] They gave her very little food, which she ate from a wooden bowl under the table. The cat and dog who ate with her were her only companions. She became the servant of the house, while the other two daughters wore pretty clothes, ate well and played with dolls.

Meanwhile Fantine found work in a factory in Montreuil owned by a man called Mr Madeleine, who had arrived in Montreuil in December 1815. He had invented a new way to make glass and became quite rich, although he lived a simple life. He used much of his money to build new hospitals and schools. He also built two new factories and employed hundreds of workers. He was kind to them and the people of the town liked him so much that they elected him mayor of the town of Montreuil.

One day Mr Madeleine saw a man in town who had had an accident; his name was Fauchelevent. A heavy cart had knocked him down and he wasn't able to get up from under the wheels. When Mr Madeleine saw this he immediately lifted the heavy cart and saved Fauchelevent's life. Everyone was amazed by Mr Madeleine's great physical strength. After this accident Fauchelevent's knee was in bad condition and he couldn't work any more, but Mr Madeleine was able to find him a job as a gardener in a convent[2] in Paris.

Only Mr Javert, the police inspector, didn't like Mr Madeleine

---

1. **rags** : dirty, old clothes that are worn thin.
2. **convent** : a place where a religious order lives.

because he was convinced that he had already seen him somewhere in the past. He thought that Mr Madeleine was dangerous criminal with a terrible past, but he never said anything about this to anyone.

Fantine liked her work at the factory and asked for news of Cosette every month. The Thénardiers always replied that she was well and happy. Unfortunately, some women at the factory discovered Fantine's secret, that she had a child although she wasn't married, and the woman in charge of the workers dismissed[3] her from her job. It was impossible for her to find work as a servant, but she was able to earn a little money sewing shirts for seventeen hours a day. She continued sending small amounts of money to the Thénardiers, but they were greedy[4] and always wanted more.

In order to save money, Fantine didn't buy wood for the fireplace in her room during the cold winter and ate very little. She soon became ill, and needed more money to send to the Thénardiers. They wanted money to buy medicine for Cosette, who wasn't feeling well. Fantine decided to sell her long, blonde hair. And then she sold her beautiful front teeth to a travelling dentist who made false teeth.

Fantine was desperate[5] because the Thénardiers demanded more and more money to look after Cosette. She cried during the night and didn't know what to do. She was weak and ill. What else could she sell? She decided that she had no other choice — she had to sell herself. So she went on the streets, waiting for men.

3. **dismissed** : sent away from a job.
4. **greedy** : when you always want more than you need.
5. **desperate** : very sad and with no hope for the future.

The text and **beyond**

1 **Comprehension check**
Answer the following questions.

1   Describe Fantine.
2   Who was Mrs Thénardier?
3   Why did Fantine leave Paris?
4   What did Fantine ask Mrs Thénardier?
5   How did Mr Thénardier react?
6   How did the Thénardiers treat Cosette?
7   Who was Mr Madeleine?
8   What happened to Fauchelevent?
9   Why didn't Mr Javert like Mr Madeleine?
10   Why did Fantine lose her job at the factory?
11   Why did Fantine become ill?
12   What did Fantine sell in order to make some money?

2 **Vocabulary**
A   Find the opposite of the following words in Chapter Two.

1   Ugly   ....
2   Poor   ....
3   Unkind   ....
4   Light   ....
5   Strong   ....
6   Destroy   ....
7   Safe   ....
8   Generous   ....
9   Attractive   ....
10   Clean   ....

B   Now write five sentences using some of the words above.

'I used to work in Paris but my husband died and I lost my job,' said Fantine.

> We use **used to** plus the base form of the verb to talk about habits in the past, for things which we always/usually/often did in the past. We don't do these things now. Look at these examples:
> *Mary **used to live** in London, but now she lives in Bristol.*
> *They **used to travel** on foot, but now they prefer to travel by horse and carriage.*
> *I **used to get up** early when I was a student.*

3 *Used to*
   Make sentences with *used to* + verb about these situations. The first is done for you.

   0   Marian worked at the library for three years. Now she's a school teacher.
       Marian used to work at the library.

   1   My sister collected stamps when she was a child.
       ....

   2   Robert is an artist now, but ten years ago he designed clothes.
       ....

   3   Brad is in prison. He robbed banks before the police caught him.
       ....

   4   I played volleyball in high school, but I now prefer to play tennis.
       ....

4 **Writing**
   Write five sentences about how life used to be 200 years ago. Then read your sentences to the class. There is an example at the beginning.

   0   *People used to travel with the horse and carriage 200 years ago.*
   1   ....
   2   ....
   3   ....
   4   ....
   5   ....

27

5 **Vocabulary**

A   Read the definition and write the word in the spaces provided.

1   A place where a religious order lives: _ _ _ _ _ _ _

2   Very sad and with no hope for the future: _ _ _ _ _ _ _ _ _

3   When you always want more than you need: _ _ _ _ _ _

4   Sent away from a job: _ _ _ _ _ _ _ _ _

5   When you want to hurt or punish someone who has hurt you:
    _ _ _ _ _ _ _

B   Now use the words from activity A to complete the sentences.

1   Mr Thénardier was a very .... man who always wanted money.

2   Jean Valjean wanted .... because of the long years at the Bagne of Toulon.

3   Fantine was .... because she had no work and no money.

4   Fauchelevent went to work as a gardener in a .... in Paris.

5   Fantine was .... from her job at the glass factory.

T: GRADE 6

6 **Speaking: travel**

Fantine walked from Paris to Montfermeil, and she will walk to Montreuil. Travel and transportation have changed a lot since then. Talk to your partner about travel and transportation and use these questions to help you.

1   How many different forms of transportation can you name?

2   What are the advantages and disadvantages of these forms of transportation.

3   What form of transportation do you prefer when you travel? Why?

4   How do people travel long distances in your country?

5   What do you think the most common form of transportation of the future will be?

7 PRELIMINARY Notices

Look at the text in each question. What does it say? Mark the correct letter — A, B or C.

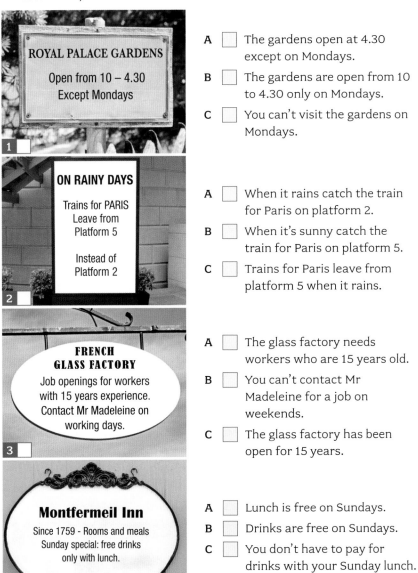

ROYAL PALACE GARDENS

Open from 10 – 4.30
Except Mondays

1

A ☐ The gardens open at 4.30 except on Mondays.

B ☐ The gardens are open from 10 to 4.30 only on Mondays.

C ☐ You can't visit the gardens on Mondays.

ON RAINY DAYS

Trains for PARIS
Leave from
Platform 5

Instead of
Platform 2

2

A ☐ When it rains catch the train for Paris on platform 2.

B ☐ When it's sunny catch the train for Paris on platform 5.

C ☐ Trains for Paris leave from platform 5 when it rains.

FRENCH
GLASS FACTORY
Job openings for workers
with 15 years experience.
Contact Mr Madeleine on
working days.

3

A ☐ The glass factory needs workers who are 15 years old.

B ☐ You can't contact Mr Madeleine for a job on weekends.

C ☐ The glass factory has been open for 15 years.

Montfermeil Inn
Since 1759 - Rooms and meals
Sunday special: free drinks
only with lunch.

4

A ☐ Lunch is free on Sundays.

B ☐ Drinks are free on Sundays.

C ☐ You don't have to pay for drinks with your Sunday lunch.

Before you read

1 PRELIMINARY Listening

Listen to the beginning of Chapter Three and choose the correct answer — A, B, or C.

1   One winter night Fantine started fighting with
    A ☐ a rich young man.
    B ☐ police inspector Javert.
    C ☐ Mr Madeleine.

2   Police inspector Javert
    A ☐ arrested Fantine.
    B ☐ arrested Mr Madeleine.
    C ☐ did not arrest Fantine.

3   Mr Madeleine took Fantine
    A ☐ to see Cosette.
    B ☐ to his home.
    C ☐ to a religious convent.

4   Police inspector Javert thought that
    A ☐ Mr Madeleine was a man called Jean Valjean.
    B ☐ Mr Madeleine was Fantine's father.
    C ☐ Mr Madeleine was a man called Champmathieu.

5   Mr Madeleine decided
    A ☐ to dismiss police inspector Javert.
    B ☐ to take Fantine to Montfermeil.
    C ☐ to go to a trial in Arras.

2 Reading pictures

Look at the picture on page 33 and answer these questions.

1   Who is sitting behind the desk?
2   Who are the men holding Fantine?
3   What do you think Fantine is saying to the man behind the desk?
4   Who is standing behind the men and Fantine?

Police inspector Javert

A few months later on a cold winter night, Fantine was on the street. A rich young man saw her and started saying horrible things to her.

'How ugly you are!' he said. 'You don't even have any front teeth! Go away and hide your ugly face!' He took some snow from the street and threw it at Fantine, who immediately attacked him. They started fighting near a café. Police inspector Javert, who was walking by, grabbed Fantine and took her to the police station. He decided to send her to prison for six months.

'Please, inspector Javert,' cried Fantine, 'I owe a hundred francs. If I don't pay, my daughter will lose her home and be out on the street. Please don't send me to prison!'

CHAPTER **THREE**

Inspector Javert listened coldly and then ordered the policemen to take her to prison. While the policemen were trying to take her away, a voice said, 'One moment please.'

Javert looked up and saw Mr Madeleine, the mayor of the town, and the owner of the glass-making factory.

'This woman must be released,' said Mr Madeleine in a firm voice.

'What!' replied Javert. 'She attacked a man in the street!'

'I saw what happened in the street,' said Mr Madeleine. 'It was the man's fault, not the woman's. You should arrest him, not her.'

Fantine recognized Mr Madeleine and shouted, 'You own the factory where I used to work. I lost my job and it's your fault! Now I've had to sell myself to men, but I didn't have a choice. I'll never see my daughter again if I don't make money.'

Javert argued with Madeleine for some time, but he finally agreed with him and did not arrest Fantine. Javert walked angrily out of the room and left the mayor and Fantine alone together.

Madeleine looked at Fantine's pale, tired face and said, 'I really didn't know that you had lost your job, but I want to help you now. I'll pay your debts and arrange for your daughter to return to you. I can give you the money you need, and you'll be happy again.'

Fantine stared at Madeleine with tears in her sad blue eyes. For the first time in her life she found a kind human being who wanted to help her and her daughter.

She fell to her knees, kissed the back of Mr Madeleine's hand and said, 'If only I had a job, I would have enough money to pay my debts and fetch my daughter.'

Fantine needed a good place to stay and Mr Madeleine took her to a convent, where she would be safe and comfortable.

CHAPTER **THREE**

Mr Madeleine sent the greedy Thénardiers 300 francs and asked them to send Cosette to Montreuil immediately. But Mr Thénardier thought that Fantine had become rich, and he demanded 500 francs. Madeleine sent the money, but Mr Thénardier found more excuses and did not send Cosette to Montreuil.

Although Fantine was happier and more comfortable now, she had a fever. Years of poverty had made her weak and ill, so that she was unable to leave her bed.

When Mr Madeleine visited Fantine she always asked, 'When will I see Cosette?'

Mr Madeleine always replied, 'Soon. Very soon.' And Fantine's eyes were filled with joy.

Mr Madeleine decided to go to Montfermeil and fetch Cosette himself. One morning while he was getting ready for the journey, an unexpected visitor walked into his office. It was inspector Javert.

'Javert, what is it?' asked Mr Madeleine, who was busy at his desk.

'Mr Madeleine, I've come to apologise,' Javert replied.

'What do you mean?' asked Mr Madeleine, confused.

'I've... I've treated you unjustly,' said Javert, looking at Mr Madeleine. 'You see, I was angry with you a few weeks ago when you told me to release that woman. So I wrote to the police headquarters in Paris and told them about you.'

'I don't understand,' said Mr Madeleine. 'Told them what about me?'

'Please forgive me, Mr Madeleine, but I thought you were a man called Jean Valjean,' said Javert, who was feeling embarrassed. 'He was a prisoner I saw twenty years ago when I worked at a prison in Toulon. After he was released from prison Valjean stole some silver from the Bishop of Digne, and the police tried to catch him but he got away. When you arrived in Montreuil I suspected that you were Jean Valjean, and when I saw you lift the cart to free that man Fauchelevent I was sure you were him, but now I know I was wrong — very wrong. I'm really sorry. You must, of course, dismiss me from my job because I don't deserve your trust.'

Mr Madeleine looked at Javert in the eyes and said calmly, 'I really don't understand.'

'Let me explain,' said Javert, nervously. 'The police headquarters in Paris told me that Jean Valjean was arrested last autumn for stealing some apples. He had changed his name to Champmathieu, but two prisoners from Toulon recognized him. I went to the prison of Arras and I saw that this man was really Jean Valjean. Of course, he said that he was innocent. His trial is tomorrow in Arras, and if he's guilty, he'll spend the rest of his life in prison.'

Mr Madeleine kept looking at the papers on his desk and said, 'Javert, I'm not interested in this matter, and I'm sure you have other work to do.'

'I'm going to the man's trial tomorrow,' said Javert, 'but after our conversation you must dismiss me. Please forgive me.'

Mr Madeleine got up and said, 'Javert, you're an honest man. You have made a mistake, but I want you to continue your excellent work as inspector of police.'

Javert left the office and Mr Madeleine stared at the papers on his desk with a strange, confused look in his eyes. That afternoon he visited Fantine, who had a high fever and a bad cough.

'Cosette?' she asked weakly.

'Soon. Very soon,' he replied softly.

Mr Madeleine stayed awake all night and thought about Javert's story. He knew that he could not let Champmathieu go to prison

for crimes he had not committed. His meeting with the kind bishop had changed him — he wanted to be a good, honest man and help others. If he went to the trial in Arras and told the truth he would lose everything he had. But this was the right thing to do, because the truth was more important than anything else. After all, *he was Jean Valjean.*

Early the next morning Mr Madeleine left for Arras and got there when the trial had already started. Champmathieu, a big, simple man, said he was innocent, but no one believed him. Several witnesses[1] declared that Champmathieu was Jean Valjean.

When the judge was ready to announce his decision, Mr Madeleine stood up, pale and trembling, and said, 'This man is not Jean Valjean. I am Jean Valjean.'

Everyone in the courtroom recognized Mr Madeleine and was shocked. At first no one believed him, but he persuaded the court of his real identity.

'And now I must leave,' Mr Madeleine said to the judge. 'I have important things to do. You know where to find me; I will not escape!'

When he had gone, the judge said to Champmathieu, who was completely confused, 'You are free to go!'

As soon as Mr Madeleine got back to Montreuil, he went to visit Fantine, who was very ill. Suddenly a man opened the door of Fantine's room — it was Javert! Poor Fantine thought he had come for her.

'Mr Madeleine, please protect me,' cried Fantine, who was terribly frightened.

---

1. **witness** : a person in a court of law who says what he/she knows about a crime.

'Don't be afraid, Fantine,' said Mr Madeleine calmly, 'he has come for me.'

Mr Madeleine turned to Javert and in a low voice said, 'Please give me three days so that I can go and fetch this woman's daughter.'

'What!' cried Javert. 'Do you think I'm stupid? You want three days to escape!'

'No, Javert!' exclaimed Mr Madeleine, angrily. 'I don't want to escape. I promised Fantine that I would go and fetch her daughter.'

Fantine heard the conversation and sat up in bed and cried, 'Fetch Cosette? What do you mean? Isn't she already here? Where's my little Cosette? I want to see her...' Then, suddenly she fell back on the pillow. She was dead.

Mr Madeleine closed Fantine's eyes and said to Javert, 'I'm ready to go now.'

Mr Madeleine looked at Fantine's body for the last time. Then he turned around and walked to the door; Javert followed him closely.

Soon everyone in town knew of Mr Madeleine's arrest. The townspeople were shocked because they knew that Mr Madeleine was a kind and honest man and an excellent mayor.

'Why did the police arrest Mr Madeleine?' asked one man. 'I've known him for five years and he's a kind and honest man.'

'And he's been an excellent mayor,' said another man. 'He's done only good things for our town.'

'Yes,' agreed another woman. 'He's given work to many people in his glass factory.'

Several days after his arrest, Jean Valjean escaped from prison during the night. Most people were not surprised to hear this and said with satisfaction, 'It certainly takes more than a prison in a small town to hold a man like that!'

The text and **beyond**

1 PRELIMINARY Comprehension check
For questions 1-5, choose the correct answer — A, B, C or D.

1 Police inspector Javert took Fantine to the police station
   A ☐ because she had stolen a hundred francs from a man.
   B ☐ because she had insulted a rich young man.
   C ☐ because she had attacked a rich young man.
   D ☐ because she had thrown snow at a rich young man.

2 Mr Madeleine decided to help Fantine
   A ☐ and went to Montfermeil to fetch Cosette.
   B ☐ but she refused his help.
   C ☐ and sent the Thénardiers 800 francs.
   D ☐ and found her a job in his factory.

3 Inspector Javert apologised to Mr Madeleine
   A ☐ because he had treated him unjustly.
   B ☐ and left his job as Police Inspector in Montreuil.
   C ☐ but told him to leave Montreuil immediately.
   D ☐ and invited him to dinner at his home.

4 Mr Madeleine went to the trial in Arras
   A ☐ but got there when the trial was over.
   B ☐ and said that he was Jean Valjean.
   C ☐ because he was a friend of Champmathieu.
   D ☐ with Inspector Javert.

5 While Mr Madeleine was visiting Fantine,
   A ☐ inspector Javert came to arrest her.
   B ☐ Cosette came to visit her mother.
   C ☐ inspector Javert arrested Jean Valjean.
   D ☐ inspector Javert came to apologise to him.

'If only I had a job, I would have enough money to pay my debts and fetch my daughter.'

We use the **second conditional** when we are thinking about a situation in the present or future which is hypothetical, unlikely or unreal. We form the second conditional like this:

If + past verb, + *would* + verb

Look at these examples:

If I had money, I would buy a new car.

If Sally studied a lot, she would pass the Maths test.

If I/he/she/it were is grammatically correct in second conditional sentences.

If she were rich, she would stop working.

BUT, in informal English, people often use ***was***: *If she was rich, she would stop working.*

2 **The second conditional**

Here are the dreams of five people. For each person, write a second conditional sentence. There is an example at the beginning.

0 **JANE:** I want to win the lottery. I want to live in the Bahamas.

...........*If Jane won the lottery, she would live in the Bahamas.*...........

1 **BILL:** I want to become a doctor. I want to help sick people.

....

2 **SUSAN:** I want to have a pony. I want to go riding every weekend.

....

3 **ALEX:** I want to go to Mars. I want to be an astronaut.

....

4 **LIZZIE:** I want to be a famous actress. I want to work in Hollywood.

....

5 **CHARLIE:** I want to phone Karen. I don't know her number.

....

'I've known him for five years and he's a kind and honest man.'

We often use the **present perfect tense** with *for* and *since*:
I have lived in Paris for eight years.
He has studied English for six months.
They have lived in Paris since April.
We have not heard from them since last year.
We use *for* when we mention the length of a period of time:
for three months... for two weeks... for an hour...
We use *since* when we mention the beginning of a period in the past:
Since April 22nd... since I was fifteen years old... since last summer...

3 **Present perfect tense with *for* and *since***
Complete these sentences with *for* or *since*.

1   Mr Thénardier has been the innkeeper .... eight years.
2   They have owned a home in the country .... September.
3   Mrs Thénardier has worked at the inn .... she was twenty years old.
4   The children have played in the park .... three hours.
5   My aunt and uncle have been on holiday in France .... six weeks.
6   He has not visited his parents .... last year.
7   They have not gone swimming .... August.
8   We have studied for the Maths test .... five hours.
9   You have not written to me............................ Christmas.
10   I have stayed at my cousin's house .... a month.

4 **Discussion**
Work in small groups and discuss these questions. Then compare your answers with the other groups in your class. In your opinion...

1   Why didn't Mr Madeleine tell police inspector Javert the truth about his identity immediately?

2 Why did he decide to go to the trial in Arras and reveal his identity?

3 Did the Bishop's words change Mr Madeleine's character?

4 What would you have done in a similar situation and why?

5 PRELIMINARY **Writing**

Jean Valjean decides to write to the kind Bishop of Digne. He wants to tell him:

- about the successful factory he set up;
- about the fact that he is mayor of the town;
- about the trial in Arras and what he plans to do;
- about how he has changed and become a kind and honest man.

Write about 80 words. Start like this:

Dear Bishop,

Many things have happened to me since I left your home years ago...

....

....

....

6 **Odd one out**

A **Circle the word that does not belong in each line. Then say what the three remaining words have in common.**

1 mayor — innkeeper — dentist — daughter

2 factory — convent — business — industry

3 silver — silk — cotton — wool

4 lawyer — judge — police — bishop

5 attractive — beautiful — plain — good looking

B **Now write five sentences using the odd words.**

Before you read

1 `PRELIMINARY` Listening

Listen to the first part of Chapter Four and choose the correct answer — A, B or C.

1 The Inn of the Sergeant of Waterloo

   A ☐ belonged to Mr Thénardier.

   B ☐ belonged to an English sergeant.

   C ☐ belonged to Mr Madeleine.

2 Cosette was now

   A ☐ ten years old.

   B ☐ eight years old.

   C ☐ six years old.

3 Cosette was sent out

   A ☐ to buy a doll at the fair.

   B ☐ to buy a bucket at the fair.

   C ☐ to get water and buy bread.

4 The huge, white-haired stranger wore

   A ☐ a long black coat.

   B ☐ a yellow hat and a black jacket.

   C ☐ a long yellow coat and a tall black hat.

5 The price of a room at the inn was

   A ☐ forty sous.

   B ☐ four sous.

   C ☐ forty francs.

2 Reading pictures

Look at the picture on page 45 and answer the following questions.

1 What is Cosette looking at?

2 Who is standing at the stall?

3 What is Cosette thinking?

CHAPTER **FOUR**

Cosette

hristmas in 1823 was lively and colourful in
the village of Montfermeil. There were plenty
of guests at the inn of the Thénardiers, which
was now known as the Inn of the Sergeant of
Waterloo. Mr Thénardier was very proud of this name. He often
told people that at Waterloo he saved the life of a wounded
general. The truth was that he didn't want to save his life but he
wanted to rob him...

Cosette, who was now eight years old, sat in her usual place
under the kitchen table and was dressed in rags.

One evening Mrs Thénardier said, 'Cosette, take this bucket
and fill it with water at the stream. And then buy some bread on
the way back. Take this coin and don't lose it! Quickly!'

CHAPTER **FOUR**

Cosette put the coin in her pocket, took the big heavy bucket and walked into the brightly lit street. She stopped in front of one of the stalls with its lights, toys and pretty objects. She was attracted by a big, beautiful doll with a long pink dress. All the little girls in Montfermeil liked this doll, but no one had enough money to buy it.

Cosette left the village, where everyone was happy and laughing, and ran down the hill into the wood. She was frightened because it was dark and cold. She put the bucket into the stream and got the water, but the coin in her pocket fell into the stream. She did not notice it, however. When the bucket was full she tried to pull it back up the hill, but it was too heavy for her tiny, frozen hands. She stopped near a tree to rest and said, 'Oh, God, please help me!'

Suddenly an enormous hand took the bucket of water from her. She looked up and saw a huge, white-haired man standing next to her. He looked strange with his tall black hat and long yellow coat, but she was not afraid of him. His eyes were kind and sad, and she trusted him.

'This bucket of water is too heavy for such a little girl,' he said gently. 'How old are you?'

'I'm eight years old, sir,' answered Cosette.

'Where are you going with this heavy bucket?' asked the white-haired man.

'I'm going to the Thénardier inn,' replied Cosette.

At this point, the white-haired man was surprised and asked, 'What's your name?'

'Cosette.'

The white-haired man looked at Cosette in amazement, picked up the heavy bucket and together they walked to the inn.

As they got close to the inn, Cosette said, 'May I have the

bucket now? If Mrs Thénardier sees that someone is helping me she'll beat me.'

As soon as the man and Cosette entered the inn, Mrs Thénardier said angrily, 'What took you so long?'

Cosette looked at her and said in a trembling voice, 'This gentleman wants a room for the night.'

Mrs Thénardier looked at his old clothes and thought, 'This man doesn't have any money to pay for a room.'

'I'm sorry, the rooms are full,' she said.

'I can pay the price of a room,' the man said.

'Forty sous,'[1] said Mrs Thénardier.

'Very well, forty sous,' said the man.

Mrs Thénardier looked at Cosette and asked, 'Where's the bread I told you to buy?'

'The baker's was shut,' Cosette lied.

'Give me back the money!' said Mrs Thénardier.

Cosette put her hand in her pocket but the coin was gone. Her thin face turned white with fear. Mrs Thénardier raised her arm to hit her, but the white-haired man stopped her.

'I've just noticed this coin on the floor,' he said, giving the coin to Mrs Thénardier. 'It probably fell out of the child's pocket.' Mrs Thénardier grabbed the coin and left the kitchen.

At that moment the door opened and two little girls appeared. Éponine and Azelma were the Thénardiers' daughters. They were two healthy girls with pink cheeks and dressed in warm winter clothes. They sat on the floor by the fire and started playing with a doll. Cosette watched them sadly. A short time later they left the doll on the floor and went to play with a big cat. Cosette looked around

---

1.   **sous** : a small former French coin of little value.

to make sure no one was watching and picked up the doll. She was happy to play with the doll, but her happiness did not last long.

Mrs Thénardier walked in and shouted, 'Cosette, who gave you permission to touch that doll with your dirty hands?'

Cosette started crying and the white-haired man saw this. He quickly left the inn and a few minutes later came back with the beautiful doll from the stall in his hands.

'Here, Cosette! It's for you!' She could hardly believe her eyes.

'Is it really for me?' asked Cosette.

The white-haired man nodded his head; he had tears in his eyes.

'I'll call her Catherine, then!' said Cosette happily.

Mrs Thénardier, Éponine, Azelma and the guests at the tables stared silently at the scene.

The next morning the white-haired man paid the bill and asked, 'How is business in Montfermeil?'

'Oh, times are very hard,' Mrs Thénardier replied. 'This is a poor country and we have so many expenses. That child, for example, costs us a lot of money. We already have two daughters to look after.'

The man thought for a moment and said, 'What would you say if I take the child from you?'

'Well, it will cost you money,' said Mrs Thénardier's husband, who was listening to the conversation.

'How much money?' asked the man.

'At least 1,500 francs,' Mr Thénardier replied happily.

The man put three 500-franc notes on the table and said, 'Now, fetch Cosette.'

As soon as Cosette had left the inn, the white-haired man bought her a black woollen dress, black stockings, a scarf and shoes. Cosette didn't know where she was going or with whom, but she felt comfortable and happy.

The text and **beyond**

1 **PRELIMINARY** **Comprehension check**

Read the summary of Chapter Four and choose the correct answer
— A, B, C or D. The first is done for you.

It was Christmas time (0) ....D.... Montfermeil, and the streets of the
village were brightly lit. There were (1) .... guests at the Inn of the
Sergeant of Waterloo. The inn belonged to the Thénardiers. Cosette,
(2) .... was a girl of eight, was dressed in rags and was treated
(3) ....

One evening Cosette had to go to fetch water at the stream. The
bucket was (4) .... heavy for her and a kind white-haired man
helped her carry it. When Cosette got (5) .... the inn Mrs Thénardier
was angry with her (6) .... she had lost a coin. The kind man gave
Mrs Thénardier a coin and she left the kitchen.

The Thénardiers' (7) .... were healthy and well dressed, and played
with a doll. Cosette had to sit under the kitchen table and (8) ....
them play.

The kind, white-haired man left the inn and want to the stalls to buy a
big, beautiful doll for Cosette. This made her very happy.

The next morning the kind man (9) .... the owner of the inn if he
could (10) .... Cosette with him. Mr Thénardier said he wanted at
least 1,500 francs, which the kind man gave him. He then (11) ....
Cosette some new clothes, and she felt happy because she could
(12) .... him.

0	**A**	over	**B**	by	**C**	on	**(D)**	in
1	**A**	many	**B**	most	**C**	much	**D**	very
2	**A**	she	**B**	that	**C**	who	**D**	which
3	**A**	terribly	**B**	poor	**C**	bad	**D**	terrible
4	**A**	plenty	**B**	too	**C**	to	**D**	enough
5	**A**	by	**B**	in	**C**	at	**D**	to
6	**A**	so	**B**	because	**C**	why	**D**	when
7	**A**	sons	**B**	nephews	**C**	daughters	**D**	nieces

8	A	watch	B	looking	C	observe	D	look
9	A	spoke	B	said	C	asked	D	talked
10	A	give	B	have	C	bring	D	take
11	A	bought	B	sold	C	fetched	D	tried on
12	A	look at	B	trust	C	talk	D	play

Cosette, who was now eight years old, sat in her usual place under the kitchen table and was dressed in rags.

When we want to add extra information to a sentence we can use a **non-defining relative clause.**

In the sentence above, the middle part starting with **who** gives us extra information which isn't essential to the main part of the sentence. Non-defining relative clauses are separated from the rest of the sentence with commas or a comma and a full stop,

Cosette left the village, where everyone was happy and laughing, and ran down the hill into the wood.

In this sentence, the middle part starting with **where** gives us extra information which isn't essential to the main part of the sentence.

2 Non-defining relative clauses

Make sentences with non-defining relative clauses using *who* or *where*. The first one is done for you.

0 My Aunt Molly lives in London. She visited me last week.
   ......*My Aunt Molly, who lives in London, visited me last week*......

1 My grandmother gave me this new watch. She's 90 years old.

2 There are 19 roller coasters at Six Flags Magic Mountain. It's my favourite amusement park.

3 Harry speaks French perfectly. He was our travel guide this summer.

4 Sue and Rob wanted to go on holiday. They were bored at home.

5 Pat's Pizza Place makes the best pizza. We ate there last night.

6 The science museum is open only on weekends. We met Sally there last week.

3 Crossword puzzle

Complete this crosswords.

Across

3 a place where a religious order lives

5

7 when you want to hurt or punish someone who has hurt you

8 send away a person

10 an important religious person in the Christian church

Down

1

2 a covered place where horses and other animals sleep

3

4 a person in a court of law who says what he/she knows about a crime

6 dirty, old clothes that are worn thin

8

9 the most important person in a town or city

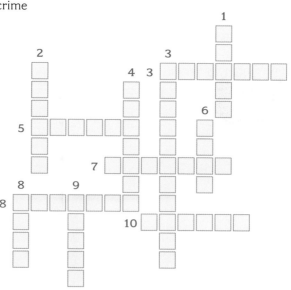

4 Surf the Net

Let's find out more about the town of Digne.
Work with a partner and answer these questions.

1 Where in France is Digne located?

2 Who were the first people to live in Digne?

3 When did Digne become a Roman town and what was its Roman name?

4 Why are its thermal waters important?

5 How many people live there today?

6 What famous flower grows in Digne?

Giuseppe Canella, Street in Paris, 1833.

Paris at the time of
King Louis-Philippe

The Paris of **King Louis-Philippe** was the city described in the novels of Victor Hugo **between 1830 and 1848**. During that time the population of Paris increased from 785,000 in 1831 to 1,053,000 in 1848. The centre of the city was very crowded. The heart of the city, around the Ile de la Cité, was a maze [1] of narrow, winding streets and old buildings from earlier centuries. It was a dark, unhealthy and often dangerous place.

The **River Seine** was a busy place with boats and barges [2] transporting goods along the river. During the summer people went swimming in the river. The city sewers emptied directly into the Seine, and people

1. **maze**:   2. **barges**:

Giuseppe Canella, L'Île de la Cité and the Pont Neuf, 1832.

threw their rubbish there. Since there were few public drinking fountains, water from the Seine was distributed by people carrying buckets from a pole on their shoulders – and people drank the dirty water!

In 1830 cholera [3] killed more than twenty thousand people. The Comte de Rambuteau, a government official, tried to improve living conditions in the centre of the city. He created stone paths near the Seine and planted trees along the river. He built a new street, now called Rue Rambuteau, to connect the **Le Marais District** with the markets, and began the construction of **Les Halles**, the famous

3. **cholera** : a serious disease caused by drinking infected water or eating infected food.

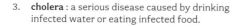

King Louis-Philippe, 1834

Claude Monet, *La gare Saint Lazare*, 1877, Musée d'Orsay, Paris, France.

central market of Paris. In August 1837 the first passenger train line travelled from Paris to Le Pecq, a small town near Saint Germain-en-Laye, which is 19 km northwest of Paris. This new train line served 18,000 passengers on its first day and it was an exciting event for everyone. The passenger train brought many changes to Parisian and French society. The middle and upper classes could now afford to travel quickly and comfortably to other parts of the country. Communications, transportation and trade greatly improved during this time.

The first railway station in Paris was Gare Saint Lazare, and then other stations were built The famous French artist Claude Monet created an important painting in 1877 called *La gare Saint Lazare*. In the late 1800's other great French artists like Édouard Manet and Gustave Caillebotte also painted railway stations in Paris.

Lipperheide, The Arc de Triomphe, Place de l'Etoile, 1848.

Howerver, the population of Paris grew, so did the anger of the working classes, who were tired of their terrible living conditions. There were many violent riots between 1830 and 1832, which Victor Hugo wrote about in *Les Misérables*. However, in spite of the riots, life for the working classes did not improve for a long time. They were the unfortunate victims of social injustice.

1 **Comprehension check**
Answer these questions.

1   Describe the centre of Paris in the 1830s.
2   What was the River Seine like?
3   How was water distributed at that time?
4   Who was Comte de Rambuteau and what did he do?
5   How long was the first railway line and where did it go?
6   How did the train change Parisian and French society?
7   How did the working classes react to their problems?

ACTIVITIES

Before you read

1 PRELIMINARY **Listening**
Listen to Chapter Five and choose the correct answer — A, B, or C.

1 What was Gorbeau House?
   A ☐ part of a convent in Paris
   B ☐ a building in Montfermeil
   C ☐ an old building in Paris

2 How long had Jean Valjean been alone in the world?
   A ☐ for more than twenty years
   B ☐ for almost nineteen years
   C ☐ for eighteen years

3 When did Jean Valjean go out?
   A ☐ in the early morning
   B ☐ in the evening
   C ☐ at night

4 Who did Jean Valjean give money to?
   A ☐ to poor children
   B ☐ to old people
   C ☐ to beggars

5 Where did Fauchelevent live?
   A ☐ near a bridge
   B ☐ at the Bernardine Convent
   C ☐ at Gorbeau House

2 **Reading pictures**
Look at the picture on page 61 and answer the following questions.

1 Where is Cosette?
2 Who are the two men in the room?
3 What are they talking about?

The convent

T he white-haired man who took Cosette away from the cruel Thénardiers was Jean Valjean. He had escaped from prison and after many adventures he had gone to Montfermeil to fetch Cosette as he had promised Fantine.

Jean Valjean arrived in Paris with Cosette asleep in his arms. He stopped outside a large, old building that was almost in ruins. It was called Gorbeau House. He took a key from his pocket, opened the old wooden door and slowly carried Cosette upstairs to the room he had rented since his escape from Montreuil. There was little furniture in the room — an old bed, a mattress on the floor, a wooden table, some chairs and a stove.[1] Valjean put Cosette on the bed without waking her.

1. stove :

CHAPTER **FIVE**

The next morning, as soon as Cosette opened her eyes she got out of bed saying, 'I'm coming, Mrs Thénardier!'

Then she saw the kind old face of Jean Valjean looking at her and she smiled at him.

'It's all true,' said Cosette. 'I thought it was just a dream.'

Cosette spent her days playing with her doll, Catherine, and singing and laughing. Valjean told her about her mother and taught her to read and write. For more than twenty years Valjean had been alone in the world. Nothing touched his heart until he met Cosette. Now he discovered happiness every time he looked at her innocent, trusting face. He had discovered love.

Valjean did not want anyone to see him so he didn't go out during the day; he walked for a few hours in the evening. Sometimes he walked with Cosette and other times he walked alone. He often gave money to beggars and one evening he gave some money to a beggar who was sitting under a streetlamp. The beggar stared at Valjean for a moment. Valjean was shocked because the beggar looked like Javert — he had the same eyes!

'It can't be Javert,' he thought. 'I must be dreaming.' When he went to bed that night he couldn't sleep. Early the next morning he heard footsteps in the corridor outside his room. He quietly went to the door and put his eye to the big keyhole [2] and saw the back of a man who was walking towards the stairs. Valjean's heart beat fast and he began to sweat. It was Javert!

He knew it was too dangerous to stay at Gorbeau House any longer, so he spent the entire day making preparations to leave. That evening he went downstairs and carefully looked up and down the dark street. It seemed empty, but he could not see into

2. **keyhole** :

the shadows behind the tall trees. He went back upstairs to get Cosette, who was waiting for him with her doll in her arms.

'Come on, Cosette,' he said, 'we must leave.'

Cosette took his hand and together they went down the stairs. Fortunately there was a full moon that night, and Valjean walked quickly along the narrow streets. When the church bells struck eleven o'clock he turned around to look back. In the light of a streetlamp he saw four men walking along the street in his direction. He and Cosette began to walk more quickly. He turned around for a moment to see the men and saw that one of them was... inspector Javert.

Poor Cosette was exhausted, so Valejan picked her up and started running across a bridge. He continued running until he came to a high wall. He could climb it alone, but how could he carry Cosette? Suddenly he had an idea. He ran to a nearby streetlight and pulled some wire from a metal box. He then tied one end of the wire around Cosette's waist, climbed the wall and pulled the little girl up. Although Valjean was very strong, it was difficult work. Luckily there was a tree behind the wall and Valjean carried Cosette down into the branches.

'He must be here!' cried Javert on the other side of the wall. 'How could he possibly escape?' But eventually Javert and his men left.

Cosette was frightened and cold, and Valjean was worried.

'I must find a safe place for Cosette,' he thought. 'But where?'

Suddenly he heard the voice of a man, and without thinking he ran to him saying, 'A hundred francs! I'll give you a hundred francs if you give me shelter for one night!'

The man turned around, looked at Valjean and cried, 'Mr Madeleine! It's you! What are you doing here?'

CHAPTER **FIVE**

'Fauchelevent!' cried Valjean, who was equally surprised. 'I saved your life years ago! And now I need your help — please help me!'

'Of course I'll help you,' said Fauchelevent. 'I'm the gardener here at the Bernardine Convent. Come with me!'

Valjean and Cosette quickly followed Fauchelevent.

A quarter of an hour later Cosette was asleep in the gardener's warm bed while Valjean and Fauchelevent ate bread and cheese and talked.

'Cosette and I need a place to stay,' said Valjean. 'I'd like to stay here at the convent. Can you help us?'

'Let me think,' said Fauchelevent. 'I'll have to ask the Mother Superior.[3] I can tell her that I'm getting old and that I need help in the garden. I can introduce you as my brother, Ultime, and I'll tell her you have a young daughter.'

'Thank you, Fauchelevent,' said Valjean softly. 'You're a true friend. I greatly appreciate your help in this moment of need.'

The next day Fauchelevent spoke to the Mother Superior, who agreed to keep Ultime and his young daughter at the convent. Life was finally easier for Valjean and Cosette. The years passed and Valjean worked in the garden of the convent, while Cosette grew up and was educated there with other young girls of fine Parisian families. She became a beautiful young lady, and she and Valjean were happy at the Bernardine Convent.

---

3.   **Mother Superior (here)** : the most important person of the convent who makes decisions.

The text and **beyond**

1 **Comprehension check**
Answer the following questions.

1   What had Jean Valjean promised Fantine?
2   Where did Jean Valjean live in Paris?
3   How did Cosette spend her days?
4   Why didn't Jean Valjean go out during the day?
5   Why did Jean Valjean and Cosette have to leave their home in Paris?
6   Who followed Jean Valjean and Cosette during the night?
7   Decribe how Valjean and Cosette escaped.
8   Who helped Jean Valjean and Cosette find shelter?
9   What did Fauchelevent tell the Mother Superior?
10   Where did Jean Valjean and Cosette live for many years and why?

2 **PRELIMINARY** **Sentence transformation**
For each question, complete the second sentence so that it means the same as the first, using no more than three words.

1   He must be hiding somewhere.
    I .... that he is hiding somewhere.

2   Jean had no time to think about the escape.
    Jean did not .... to think about the escape.

3   When do you plan to take your holiday in France?
    When are you .... take your holiday in France?

4   There were few shops in the neighbourhood.
    There .... shops in the neighbourhood.

5   We can't do that.
    We .... to do that.

6   The gardener borrowed some money from Jean Valjean.
    Jean Valjean .... the gardener some money.

3 PRELIMINARY Notices

Look at the text in each question. What does it say? Mark the correct letter — A, B or C.

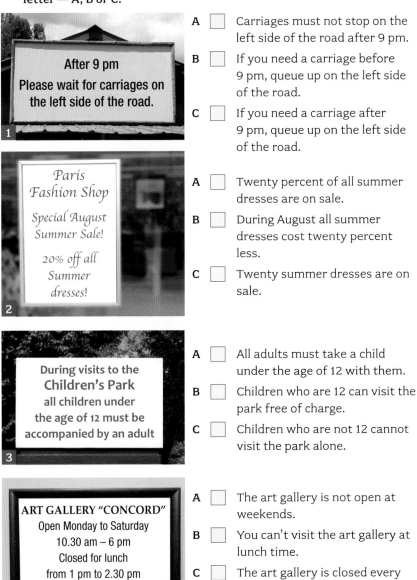

1

After 9 pm
Please wait for carriages on
the left side of the road.

A ☐ Carriages must not stop on the left side of the road after 9 pm.

B ☐ If you need a carriage before 9 pm, queue up on the left side of the road.

C ☐ If you need a carriage after 9 pm, queue up on the left side of the road.

2

Paris
Fashion Shop

Special August
Summer Sale!

20% off all
Summer
dresses!

A ☐ Twenty percent of all summer dresses are on sale.

B ☐ During August all summer dresses cost twenty percent less.

C ☐ Twenty summer dresses are on sale.

3

During visits to the
Children's Park
all children under
the age of 12 must be
accompanied by an adult

A ☐ All adults must take a child under the age of 12 with them.

B ☐ Children who are 12 can visit the park free of charge.

C ☐ Children who are not 12 cannot visit the park alone.

4

ART GALLERY "CONCORD"
Open Monday to Saturday
10.30 am – 6 pm
Closed for lunch
from 1 pm to 2.30 pm

A ☐ The art gallery is not open at weekends.

B ☐ You can't visit the art gallery at lunch time.

C ☐ The art gallery is closed every afternoon.

The big stores of *La Belle Jardinière* during the works of Haussmann in Paris, 1867.

Haussmann and the *renovation*[1] *of Paris*

In 1852 Emperor Napoleon III asked the French architect Georges-Eugène Haussmann (1809-1891) to renovate Paris – to make it a cleaner, safer and more modern city. This was the beginning of the renovation of Paris that went on until the early 1900s.

The Industrial Revolution

The Industrial Revolution of the late 1700s and early 1800s had brought advancements in technology. Many people went to work in Paris and other French cities, and this meant that a lot of new houses had to be built. French society was changing rapidly. There were many more things to produce and sell. Therefore, all kinds of shops and factories started opening all over the city, which needed better planning and improved distribution of space.

1. **renovation** : when something is rebuilt or made new and better.

Haussmann's projects to renew Paris

Between 1853 and 1870 Haussmann knocked down crowded, unhealthy medieval neighbourhoods and built new, wide streets with tall trees called boulevards and avenues. The traffic problem was solved thanks to the rebuilding of the city streets. Beautiful new parks with fountains, flowers and artificial lakes, like the Bois de Boulogne and Bois de Vincennes, were created for the public.

New, spacious squares like Place de la Republique were built. Haussmann also designed and constructed new public buildings, bridges, hospitals, churches and theatres. Transportation by train was becoming very popular and Paris needed new train stations, which Haussmann created: the Gare du Nord and the Gare de l'Est.

The city's sewers, water pipes and tunnels were in terrible condition and he rebuilt them and made drinking water safe for people to drink. Many Parisians did not like what Haussmann was doing because their routine was upset by all the work that was going on in the city. Everything was changing. But when they started seeing the wonderful results, they changed their minds. The appearance of Paris today is a result of Haussmann's brilliant planning and hard work.

1 **Comprehension check**
Answer the following questions.

1 What did Emperor Napoleon III ask Haussmann to do?
2 Why did Paris need to be renovated?
3 How did Haussmann change the neighbourhoods of Paris?
4 Why did Paris need new train stations?
5 Why were many Parisians against Haussmann's projects?
6 What was your city or town like in the 1800s?

Before you read

1 **PRELIMINARY** Listening

Listen to the beginning of Chapter Six and choose the correct answer — A, B, and C.

1 Who was Marius's father?
   A ☐ a poor soldier
   B ☐ a drunk
   C ☐ a brave officer

2 What did George Pontmercy leave his son?
   A ☐ a small amount of money
   B ☐ a letter
   C ☐ a sword from the Battle of Waterloo

3 Where did Marius work?
   A ☐ at the Gorbeau House
   B ☐ at the Luxembourg Gardens
   C ☐ at a bookshop

4 Why did Marius become very upset?
   A ☐ because his grandfather died
   B ☐ because the young girl at the gardens disappeared
   C ☐ because he lost his job

5 What was inside the package that Marius found on the street?
   A ☐ some letters
   B ☐ some money
   C ☐ a book

2 Reading pictures

Look at the picture on page 71 and answer the following questions.

1 Who are the people in the picture?
2 What is the room like?
3 What is the old man on the left saying to his guests?

Marius

ight years had passed since Jean Valjean and Cosette arrived at the convent of the Bernardines. New people, called the Jondrettes, were now living at the old Gorbeau House. They were a very poor family — a father, a mother, two daughters and a son. A young man named Marius had recently moved into the Gorbeau House, too.

Marius was an orphan who had grown up with his grandfather, Mr Gillenormand. His grandfather had always told him that his father was a poor soldier and a drunk, who had abandoned him after his mother's death. For many years Marius believed this story, but when he was seventeen years old he learnt the truth. His father was a brave officer who had fought for Napoleon and nearly died at the Battle of Waterloo, who had loved him and his mother very much. Without telling his grandfather, Marius tried to contact his father and discovered where he was living. He

immediately went to visit him, but when he arrived he was told that his father had just died. George Pontmercy died in poverty and the only thing that he left his son was a letter:

> *For my son. My life was saved at Waterloo by a sergeant. His name was Thénardier. I believe that he recently managed a small inn in the village of Montfermeil, not far from Paris. If you ever find this man, I want you to help him in any way you can.*

Marius returned to Paris but he continued to visit his father's tomb without telling his grandfather. One day his grandfather found out what Marius was doing and got very angry. They quarreled[1] a lot and Mr Gillenormand ordered Marius to leave his house forever.

Marius now lived in a small room in the old Gorbeau House — the same room where Valjean and Cosette had lived eight years before. He worked in a bookshop and didn't earn very much money. His grandfather tried to send him money but Marius always returned it. He hated his grandfather because he had treated his poor father in a cruel way. Although life was hard for Marius, he did not forget the promise he had made his father: find Thénardier, the man who had saved his father's life, and help him.

Marius was a handsome young man but he was very shy. He went on daily walks to the beautiful Luxembourg Gardens, where for about a year Marius had noticed an old man with a lovely young girl always sitting on the same bench. One day he looked closely at the girl and thought, 'What a beautiful girl! What splendid blue eyes!' and fell in love with her. The next day Marius wore his best clothes and went back to the Luxembourg Gardens. He walked around slowly and kept looking at the girl until their eyes met. The girl fell in love with Marius, too. However, they could only see each

1. **quarreled** : argued angrily.

Marius

other at a distance at the Gardens. Since the old man had white hair, Marius called him Mr Leblanc. [2]

Two weeks later the old man and the young girl disappeared from the Luxembourg Gardens. Marius was extremely upset and tried to find out the girl's name and where she lived, but without success. He became very sad and looked all over Paris for the girl he loved, but he couldn't find her. Life had no meaning for him any more.

Summer and autumn passed and winter came, but Marius still could not find the girl he loved. One evening in February while Marius was walking along the street, two young girls dressed in rags ran into him. He looked at them as they disappeared round a corner and noticed a small package on the street.

'One of the girls probably dropped this package,' he thought, putting it in his pocket.

When Marius got home he opened the package and found four letters inside. The letters were addressed to different people and they all asked for money. He put the package with the letters in a corner of his room and went to bed.

The next morning someone knocked at Marius's door. It was a very thin girl, who looked poor and ill.

'What can I do for you?' asked Marius.

'I've got a letter for you, Mr Marius,' said the girl.

Marius took the letter and started to read it:

> My kind neighbour, my oldest daughter will tell you that my wife is ill and none of us have had any food for four days. Please, sir, you have a good heart, so please help us!
> Yours truly, Jondrette

'This letter is exactly like the others in the small package,'

2. **Leblanc** : in French the word 'blanc' means white.

69

thought Marius. 'These people are even poorer than me and they ask others for money.' He was confused.

'I think this package belongs to you,' he said, giving the girl the package with the letters.

'Oh, thank you! We lost this package last night' said the girl, running out of the room.

After his conversation with the girl from the next room, Marius stared at the wall that separated him from the poor family next door. He noticed that in the top corner near the ceiling there was a small hole. He stood up on a chair and put his eye to the hole.

'Let's see what these people are like, and how I can help them,' he thought, as he looked through the hole.

The Jondrettes' room was dirty and smelly. A man with a long, grey beard was sitting at an old table, writing a letter. A large woman was sitting by the fire, while a thin child sat on one of the beds.

Sudddenly the girl who had come to Marius's room ran into the room: 'He's coming!' she cried excitedly.

'Who's coming?' asked her father.

'The generous old man who goes to church,' replied the girl. 'I saw him with his daughter and gave him the letter. He's following me. I ran ahead to tell you.'

'Good!' exclaimed her father. 'Quickly, put out the fire and break that window! When he sees how poor we are he'll give us a lot of money.'

A minute later there was a knock at the door and Mr Jondrette opened it. 'Please come in, sir!'

An old man and a young girl entered the room and Marius, who was still looking through the hole in the wall, could not believe his eyes. It was the beautiful young girl from the Luxembourg Gardens with Mr LeBlanc. He stared at her lovely face in amazement.

The old man put a package on the old table and said, 'There are woollen blankets and warm clothes inside.'

'You're very generous, sir. Thank you!' said Mr Jondrette. 'As you can see, we have nothing. My poor wife and my son Gavroche are ill in bed. And I must pay the rent tomorrow, otherwise we must leave this room. I need sixty francs, sir.'

'Don't worry,' said the old man, 'I'll take my daughter home and come back this evening with more money for you.'

'Oh, thank you, sir! Thank you!' said Mr Jondrette.

Marius jumped down from the chair and ran out into the street. But he was too late — their carriage had already left. He went back upstairs and met the Jondrette girl in the corridor.

'What do you want?' said Marius angrily.

'What's the matter?' asked the girl, who liked Marius. 'Is there something I can do for you?'

'The old man who was here — do you know where he lives?' asked Marius.

'No, I don't; but I can find out, and then I'll tell you,' said the girl, going back to her room.

Marius sat down on his bed and buried his face in his hands. He had to find the girl he loved. Suddenly he heard a loud voice from the other room.

'I recognized him,' cried Jondrette. 'I'm sure it's him.'

When Marius heard this he jumped onto the chair and looked again through the hole in the wall.

'Are you sure?' asked his wife, who was confused.

'Of course I'm sure,' insisted Jondrette. 'I saw him eight years ago but I recognized him at once. And his daughter is Cosette. Remember little Cosette?'

His wife was shocked, 'What? That lovely young lady is... Cosette?'

'Yes, she is! Now, listen to me,' said Jondrette. 'Fortunately, he didn't recognize me, maybe because I have this long beard now. He'll be here at six o'clock with the money. I'll bring some friends of mine here to help us and we'll make sure he gives us a lot more money.'

Marius heard the entire conversation and understood that Jondrette was planning to take as much money as he could from Mr Leblanc. He had to save Mr Leblanc. But, how? There was only one thing he could do: tell the police.

Marius quickly went to the nearest police station and talked to the police inspector, Mr Javert. He told him about the day's events. When he told Javert his address he noticed that the inspector's eyes lit up with great interest.

'Go back to your room and hide there!' said Javert. 'Look at everything that's happening in the other room through the hole in the wall. When things get dangerous, just shout and we'll come immediately. We'll surprise them!'

'Very well,' said Marius, leaving the inspector's office in a hurry.

Marius went back home and at six o'clock he got onto the chair and started looking through the hole in the wall. He saw Mr Leblanc come into the Jondrettes' room and sit at the table. After a few minutes four big men walked into the dark room.

Mr Leblanc looked at them; he obviously didn't trust them. 'Who are these men?' he asked.

'They're... some friends of mine,' said Mr Jondrette, nervously.

Mr Leblanc got up from his chair and looked around the room. He knew he was in danger.

CHAPTER **SIX**

Suddenly Jondrette looked at him and said, 'You don't recognize me, do you?'

'No, I don't,' said Mr Leblanc.

'My name isn't Jondrette, it's Thénardier. I was the innkeeper at Montfermeil! You came and fetched Cosette because you had a lot of money. Now I'm poor, but I was a brave French soldier and a hero! I saved the life of a general at Waterloo... But all this has been forgotten. Now what I want is your money — *a lot of money*!'

The four men moved dangerously close to Mr LeBlanc and were ready to attack him.

When Marius heard this, his heart jumped in his chest. '*Thénardier,*' he thought, 'that's the name of the man who saved my father's life at Waterloo. That's the man I promised to help! What should I do? Call the police and save Mr Leblanc or keep the promise to my father?'

Marius didn't have time to make a choice, because Javert and his men, who were impatient, pushed open the door of the Jondrettes' room and arrested everyone. There was a lot of confusion and Mr LeBlanc, managed to open the window and disappeared into the dark.

'Where's the old man with the white hair who was in danger?' shouted Javert. Then he saw the open window and cried angrily, 'He's the cleverest of them all!'

The text and **beyond**

1 **Comprehension check**

Match the phrases in column A (1-11) with the phrases in column B (A-M) to make complete sentences. There are two phrases in column B that you do not need to use.

A

1. ☐ Marius's grandfather never told him the truth
2. ☐ George Pontmercy left his son a letter
3. ☐ Marius and his grandfather quarrelled a lot
4. ☐ At the Luxembourg Gardens Marius and a beautiful young girl
5. ☐ One day Mr Leblanc and the beautiful young girl
6. ☐ The Jondrette family wrote letters to people
7. ☐ One day Marius saw Mr Leblanc and the beautiful girl
8. ☐ Mr Jondrette, who was really Mr Thénardier,
9. ☐ Jondrette planned to call his friends to help him
10. ☐ Marius heard Jondrette's plan
11. ☐ Inspector Javert and his men

B

A disappeared from the Luxembourg Gardens.

B about his mother.

C riding in a carriage.

D through a small hole in the wall.

E about his father.

F recognized Cosette and Mr Leblanc.

G and Marius had to leave the house forever.

H and immediately told police inspector Javert.

I saw each other and fell in love.

J in which he told him about a sergeant called Thénardier.

K entered Jondrette's room and arrested everyone except Mr Leblanc.

L in which they asked for money.

M get a lot of money from Mr Leblanc.

Eight years had passed since Jean Valjean and Cosette arrived at the convent of the Bernardines.

The **past perfect simple** is used to show that something was completed or finished before another action began. It is often used in stories to give the background.

The past perfect simple is formed in this way: **had/hadn't + past participle.**

He hated his grandfather because he had treated his poor father in a cruel way.

2 The past perfect simple
Use the correct verb tense, either the past simple or the past perfect simple, to complete these sentences.

1   He (*write*) .... the letter to his son after he (*meet*) .... the sergeant.
2   Cosette (*buy*) .... the dress after she (*ask*) .... Mr Leblanc.
3   The young soldier (*marry*) .... the girl before he (*go*) .... to war.
4   They (*study*) .... the maps before they (*explore*) .... the island.
5   The child (*be*) .... afraid of water because he (*have*) .... a bad experience at the sea.
6   I (*choose*) .... this book because I (*see*) .... the play last week and liked it.
7   We (*decide*) .... to visit Paris because we (*hear*) .... so much about it.
8   He (*know*) .... his way around the city because he (*spend*) .... many years there.
9   The gardener (*have*) .... a lot of experience because he (*work*) .... at the Luxembourg Gardens for twenty years.
10 The policeman (*arrest*) .... the thief because he (*steal*) .... jewels from the Royal Palace many years ago.

3 Writing

Read the text and fill in the gaps with the words in the box.

army   people   capital   built   buildings   centre (x2)
settlements   today   largest   town

The origins of Paris

Between 250 and 225 BCE the Parisii, a group of **(1)** ...., settled on a small island in the River Seine. **(2)** .... that island is called Île de la Cité. The Parisii **(3)** .... a fort and bridges to the other banks of the Seine. Soon they began to trade with other **(4)** .... in Europe.

In the year 52 BCE the Roman **(5)** .... defeated the Parisii and set up the Roman **(6)** .... of Lutetia, which became an important **(7)** ....

The Romans built roads, homes, a theatre and other beautiful **(8)** .... The Romans changed the name of the town to Paris in 360 CE. In 508 CE Clovis I, King of the Franks, invaded Paris and made it his **(9)** ....

During the Middle Ages Paris was the **(10)** .... city in Europe. It became an important religious and commercial **(11)** ....

The University of Paris was set up on the left bank of the Seine in 1215. This university was one of the first in all of Europe. Paris suffered from the Hundred Years War in the 15th century. The city became the book-publishing capital of Europe in the 16th century.

77

The Luxembourg Gardens, Paris, France.

Beautiful gardens in Paris

The Luxembourg Gardens

The beautiful **Luxembourg Gardens**, which have a long and interesting history, are probably the most popular park in Paris. This is where Parisians and tourists go to relax and enjoy the many beauties of the park.

The Luxembourg Palace, Paris, France.

Marie de Medici

In 1611 the Italian Marie de Medici, widow of King Henry IV, decided to build a beautiful palace similar to the Pitti Palace in her native city, Florence. She bought the **Petit-Luxembourg Palace** and then began building a new one nearby. In 1612 she planted 2,000 elm[1] trees and asked Tommaso Francini, a famous garden artist, to design and build the park. Francini also designed the famous Medici Fountain, which is still a major attraction today.

After Marie de Medici's death, other monarchs neglected the Luxembourg Gardens, but after the French Revolution of the late 18th century, the gardens were restored to their original beauty.

In the late 19th century the Luxembourg Gardens had a marionette[2] theatre, a music kiosk, greenhouses, a rose garden, and a fruit orchard and about 70 statues. Around the central green lawn there are 20 statues of famous French queens and other French women.

1. **elm :**

2. **marionette :**

The Luxembourg Gardens, Paris, France.

The Luxembourg Gardens in Popular Culture

The Gardens were featured in *Les Misérables* as the meeting place of Cosette and Marius. The American writer Henry James also used the Luxembourg Gardens in his novel *The Ambassadors*.

Paris is a very green city with 421 parks and about 250,000 trees. Other splendid parks are the Bois de Vincennes, the largest park in Paris, the Bois de Boulogne and the Tuileries Gardens.

The Bois de Vincennes

This huge public park is located on the eastern side of Paris. It has four beautiful lakes where you can rent a boat and visit the lake. You can also go fishing on the lakes. There are many grassy fields where you can sit, read a book or just relax.

In the past, the kings of France considered this area their royal hunting grounds. The Olympic Summer Games of 1900 were held at the Bois de Vincennes.

The Bois de Vincennes, Paris, France.

Today there is an interesting tropical aquarium at the park, with more than 5,000 sea creatures. There's a lot to see at Bois de Vincennes, including a zoo!

1 Comprehension check

Are the following sentences true (T) or false (F)? Correct the false ones.

		T	F
1	Marie de Medici built the Pitti Palace in Florence, her native city.	☐	☐
2	The famous Medici Fountain was designed by Tommaso Francini.	☐	☐
3	During the French Revolution the Luxembourg Gardens were destroyed.	☐	☐
4	Today there are about 90 statues in the Gardens.	☐	☐
5	The Luxembourg Gardens are bigger than the Bois de Vincennes.	☐	☐
6	The Bois de Vincennes was once a royal hunting ground.	☐	☐

Rue¹ Plumet

Marius decided to leave Gorbeau House for two reasons. First of all, he greatly disliked the Jondrette family and their dishonest way of life. Secondly, he did not want to testify² against Thénardier, who was now in prison. He went to live with his friend Courfeyrac.

But Marius always thought about the beautiful girl he had met at the Luxembourg Gardens and loved so dearly.

'What's her name? Where is she? Why can't I find her?' he constantly asked himself. He was so concerned with the girl he

---

1. **rue** : French word for *street*.
2. **testify** : to speak in a court of law against someone.

loved that he didn't notice the big political problems in Paris. King Louis-Philippe was in power, but there were many people against him. Enjolras and Marius's other friends belonged to secret groups that were against the king.

One day while Marius was taking a walk and thinking about the girl he loved, he heard a familiar voice. He looked up and saw Éponine, Thénardier's oldest daughter, who was out of prison because of her young age.

'I have the address that you want,' she said, looking seriously at Marius.

'What!' exclaimed Marius, who was wild with excitement. 'The address... tell me!'

'Come with me,' said Éponine. 'I'll take you, because I don't know the street or the number.'

Marius grabbed her arm and said, 'Promise me that you'll never tell your father the address!'

'My father's in prison,' she said sadly.

Éponine took Marius to a small house with a large garden. When the old gardener Fauchelevent died, Jean Valjean and Cosette left the convent. Valjean decided to buy this house in Rue Plumet where he and Cosette could live comfortably and safely. However, Valjean didn't go out often because the police were still looking for him. He rented two other apartments in Paris so that he could hide there in case of danger. Cosette spent a lot of time in the lovely garden, sitting on a stone bench. She often thought about the young man she had fallen in love with at the Luxembourg Gardens.

One evening in April, Jean Valjean went out for a walk, leaving Cosette alone at home. She went to the garden and noticed an envelope on the bench under a stone. She quickly opened the envelope and found love letters from Marius. She ran into the house and went to her room where she read the romantic letters again and again. She fell asleep thinking about the beautiful words Marius had written to her.

The next evening Cosette was home alone again and went to the garden, where she heard a noise. She turned around and saw… Marius! She couldn't believe her eyes.

'Excuse me for coming here,' said Marius excitedly, 'but I had to see you. Please don't be afraid. Do you recognize me? Do you remember the day when you first looked at me in the Luxembourg Gardens? Perhaps I'm annoying you… but the truth is I can't live without you! Have you read my letters?'

'Oh, yes, yes!' said Cosette excitedly. 'I've read your letters many times.'

'Do you love me too?' asked Marius, looking at Cosette's beautiful blue eyes.

'Yes, I do,' replied Cosette happily.

Marius and Cosette kissed each other. Afterwards they sat together on the stone bench and asked each other many questions. They talked about their hopes and their dreams. Finally Cosette asked, 'What's your name?'

'My name's Marius. And yours?'

'Cosette.'

After this wonderful evening, Marius and Cosette always met in the garden. They held hands and talked, or just looked into each other's eyes; they were deeply in love.

One evening Marius found Cosette sitting unhappily in the garden.

'What's the matter?' asked Marius, who was worried.

'My father said that we have to leave for England,' said Cosette sadly.

CHAPTER **SEVEN**

Marius became pale and could not speak; his heart beat fast and he felt dizzy. [3]

'Cosette, my love,' said Marius, 'you can't go, you can't leave me!'

'What else can I do?' said Cosette, her voice trembling.

'I can't live without you!' exclaimed Marius.

Suddenly Cosette exclaimed, 'Wait! I have an idea! You must come too. I'll tell you where, and you must meet me there.'

'How can I possibly go to England?' said Marius, holding Cosette's hands. 'I don't have any money. Look at me — I wear a cheap hat and an old jacket, and there are holes in my boots. I'm a poor man!'

Cosette looked at the man she loved and started crying.

'Please don't cry!' said Marius. 'Listen, I have a plan. I won't come here tomorrow.'

'Why not?' said Cosette, drying her tears. 'A whole day without seeing you — that's impossible!'

'It's worth losing a day if we want to be happy forever,' said Marius, looking at Cosette's beautiful face.

'I don't understand,' said Cosette. 'What are you going to do?'

'I'll tell you the day after tomorrow,' said Marius with a strange look in his eyes. 'Trust me!'

'Alright, I won't ask any questions,' said Cosette. 'But you must promise to come here early the day after tomorrow.'

'I promise, my love,' said Marius.

The next day Marius went to see his grandfather, Mr Gillenormand. As soon as the old man saw Marius he asked, 'Why have you come here? Have you come to apologise? Do you now see that you were wrong?'

---

3. **dizzy** : when you feel that your head is spinning and you might fall down.

'No,' said Marius, seriously, 'I've come to ask your permission to get married.'

'So you want to get married at the age of twenty-one. Have you got a good job? Perhaps you've made a fortune...'

'No,' replied Marius.

'Well, then the girl is rich,' said the grandfather, raising his voice.

'No, she's not, but I want to marry her,' said Marius nervously.

'Hmm... you don't have a job and you don't have any money, but you want to get married,' said the grandfather angrily.

'Yes,' said Marius. 'Please give me your permission to marry the girl I love.'

'I will never give you my permission,' shouted Mr Gillenormand angrily. '*Never!*'

Marius was desperate and walked towards the door saying, 'I'll never ask you for anything again! Good-bye!'

The next evening Marius went to see Cosette, as he had promised. But when he got to Rue Plumet Cosette and Jean Valjean had already left, without leaving their address.

'Where can they possibly be?' Marius asked himself. Then he heard a familiar voice say, 'Mr Marius, your friends are waiting for you at the barricade⁴ in Rue de la Chanvrerie.' He turned around and saw Éponine running away into the night.

---

4.   **barricade** : a barrier in the street made with the nearest available objects.

The text and **beyond**

1 PRELIMINARY **Comprehension check**
For each question choose the correct answer — A, B, C or D.

1   Marius left his room at the Gorbeau House
   A ☐   and went to live with his grandfather.
   B ☐   because he had no money and could not pay the rent.
   C ☐   because he didn't like the Jondrette family and didn't want
          to testify against Thénardier.
   D ☐   and decided to leave Paris.

2   Enjolras and Marius's other young friends
   A ☐   were in the city prison.
   B ☐   belonged to secret groups that were against the king.
   C ☐   went to visit Thenardier's oldest daughter, Éponine.
   D ☐   lived in the Gorbeau House.

3   When Fauchelevent died, Jean Valjean and Cosette
   A ☐   left Paris because the city was not safe for them.
   B ☐   remained at the Bernardine convent.
   C ☐   went back to the Gorbeau House.
   D ☐   went to live in Rue Plumet.

4   How did Cosette get Marius's love letters?
   A ☐   She found them under a stone on the garden bench.
   B ☐   Éponine brought them to her at night.
   C ☐   Enjolras gave them to her while she was at the market.
   D ☐   She found them outside the door of her house.

5   Marius and Cosette loved each other
   A ☐   and they decided to run away together.
   B ☐   but she had to leave for England with her father.
   C ☐   but Marius did not want to marry her.
   D ☐   but she could not marry a poor man.

6   Marius want to visit his grandfather Mr Gillenormand
   A ☐   because the old man was very ill.
   B ☐   because he wanted his permission to get married.
   C ☐   because he wanted some money so he could get married.
   D ☐   because he wanted to invite him to his wedding.

2 Vocabulary

A Read the definitions. What is the word for each one? There is one space for each letter in the word.

1 Without any hope: d _ _ _ _ _ _ _ _

2 When you feel that your head is spinning and you might fall down: d _ _ _ _

3 To speak in a court of law against someone: t _ _ _ _ _ _

4 A barrier made with the nearest available objects: b _ _ _ _ _ _ _ _

5 An important person in the Christian church: b _ _ _ _ _

6 The French word for street: r _ _

7 Argued angrily: q _ _ _ _ _ _ _ _

8 Small former French coin of little value: s _ _ _

9 Sadness, suffering, despair: m _ _ _ _ _

10 Very important and significant : p _ _ _ _ _ _ _ _ _

B Now write seven sentences using the words above.

1 The .... of Digne, who was a kind and generous man, helped Jean Valjean become a better person.

2 Fantine was very tired and hungry because she had not eaten for two entire days, so she suddenly felt .... and fell on the street.

3 Fantine was .... because she didn't have any money or a job, and she couldn't send money to the Thénardiers.

4 Jean Valjean paid Mrs Thénardier forty .... for the room at the inn.

5 Marius went to visit his grandfather, Mr Gillenormand, and they .... a lot because the grandfather did not give him permission to marry Cosette.

6 Jean Valjean and Cosette lived in a house on .... Plumet.

7 Marius did not want to .... against Mr Jondrette, who was really Mr Thénardier.

8 Victor Hugo wrote about the poor and the working class in Paris that lived in ....

9 Éponine told Marius that all his friends were waiting for him at the .... in Rue de la Chanvrerie.

10 Victor Hugo was elected to the .... French Academy in Paris.

3 **Writing**

Read the text below and fill in the gaps with the words in the box.

shocked	translated	travelled	masterpiece	influenced
	realism	founders	inspired	important	

Important French Writers of the 1800s

Romanticism

Alexandre Dumas (father) was born in Villers-Cotterêts, Aisne, France, on 28 July 1802, the same year as Victor Hugo. He, too, was a Romantic writer.

Two of his best-known works are *The Count of Monte Cristo* (1844) and *The Three Musketeers* (1844). Dumas's famous works have been (1) .... into nearly one hundred languages. His wonderful books have (2) .... many successful films and plays.

In the 1840s he founded the Historical Theatre in Paris. Dumas died on 5 December 1870 and was buried at the Panthéon in Paris, a place reserved for very (3) .... people.

Realism

The expression Realism means writing the truth about familiar, every day things as they really are. Honoré de Balzac, who was born on 20 May 1799 in Tours, France, is considered one of the (4) .... of literary realism in Europe.

Balzac's (5) .... is *La Comédie Humaine* (1845), which represents a realistic view of French life in the years after the 1815 fall of Napoleon Bonaparte. His other well-known novels are *Le Père Goriot* and *Eugénie Grandet*. Balzac's writing (6) .... great writers like Émile Zola, Charles Dickens, Gustave Flaubert and Oscar Wilde. He died on 18 August 1850 and is buried at Pére Lachaise Cemetery in Paris.

Gustave Flaubert, who was born in Rouen, France, on 12 December 1821, was one of the important exponents of literary realism in Europe. His most famous novel was *Madame Bovary* (1857), the story of an unhappy marriage that initially (7) .... its readers because of its (8) ....

Flaubert (9) .... a lot during his life, visiting Greece, the Middle East and northern Africa. He died on 8 May 1880 in Rouen, the city where he was born.

⑨ ④ PRELIMINARY Listening

Listen to the guide tour talk about the Paris Opera House. Then choose
the correct answer A, B, or C.

1   The Paris Opera House is also known as

    A ☐   the Opera Palace.

    B ☐   the Garnier Palace.

    C ☐   Napoleon's Palace.

2   In what year did the Paris Opera House open?

    A ☐   in 1875

    B ☐   in 1862

    C ☐   in 1870

3   Which architectural style is not included in the opera house
building?

    A ☐   Renaissance

    B ☐   Medieval

    C ☐   Baroque

4   Who was responsible for the project of rebuilding and renovating
central Paris?

    A ☐   Marc Chagall

    B ☐   Charles Garnier

    C ☐   Georges-Eugène Haussmann

5   Why was an underground lake created?

    A ☐   for the musical *The Phantom of the Opera*

    B ☐   to make the foundations of the building safe

    C ☐   because the theatre needed a water supply

6   Who decorated the enormous dome?

    A ☐   Charles Garnier

    B ☐   Georges-Eugène Haussmann

    C ☐   Marc Chagall

Before you read

1 **The June Rebellion of 1832**
Complete the text with the words in the box below.

people (x3)	difficult	political	living
against	soldiers	poor	food

Serious economic, social and **(1)** .... problems led to the June Rebellion of 1832, which took place on 5 and 6 June. Farmers had had a **(2)** .... harvest for several years and there was very little **(3)** ....
The cost of **(4)** .... had increased and this made life **(5)** .... for the poor and the working classes. In the spring of 1832 more than 18,000 **(6)** .... died during a cholera[1] epidemic.

King Louis-Philippe had become very unpopular with students, the poor and the working classes, and so they decided to revolt[2] **(7)** .... him. Angry **(8)** .... started building barricades and fighting in the streets, but the king's **(9)** .... stopped the revolt and many **(10)** .... were killed.

2 **Prediction**
Work with a partner and answer these questions. Then present your answers to the class and compare them.

1 What do you think will happen at the barricades?
2 How will Marius find Cosette?
3 Who will Marius meet at the barricades?

1. **cholera epidemic** : a serious disease that kills many people, caused by drinking dirty water or eating bad food.
2. **revolt** : fight against the authorities of the state or kingdom.

The barricade

**M**arius hurried to Rue de la Chanvrerie to join his friends. 'I'll never see my love again,' he thought. 'I can't live without Cosette. Perhaps it's best to die!' He could hear screaming and the sound of guns in the distance.

Soldiers loyal to the king and rebels were shooting at each other; dead and wounded men lay on the streets near the barricades.

A young boy dressed in rags was running towards the barricade shouting, 'Let's fight, everyone!'. It was Gavroche, the son of the Thénardiers.

Marius's friends Enjolras, Courfeyrac and Combeferre were busy building a barricade near the *Corinthe*, an inn. Everyone in the area was building barricades, even little Gavroche.

When it got dark Enjolras said, 'Gavroche, you're so small that no one can see you. Leave the barricades and go along the walls and into the streets and then come back and tell me what you've seen.'

'Alright,' said Gavroche, 'but take a look at that man over there. He's a spy!'

Enjolras and four other men approached the man and asked, 'Who are you?'

The man stared at Enjolras and replied in a low voice, 'I'm part of the city government.'

'What's your name?'

'Javert.'

Enjolras was angry and said to one of his men, 'Tie him to one of the columns¹ of the building.'

As soon as Enjolras saw Marius he threw his arms around his neck.

'So you've come to fight with us!' cried Enjolras. 'Good!'

After two months of happiness with Cosette, Marius was now in the middle of a revolt and he couldn't believe this was happening to him. He was ready to fight for the Republic, but suddenly he heard a weak voice calling his name from the shadows.

'Mr Marius!'

He turned around and saw a dark shape on the ground near him. A pale face looked at him and asked, 'Do you recognize me? I'm Éponine.'

Marius bent down and saw that it was poor little Éponine, dressed in man's clothes.

1. **column** :

'What are you doing here?' asked Marius. 'And what's happened to your hand?'

'A soldier was going to shoot you, but I put my hand in front of his gun,' said Éponine in a low voice. 'The bullet[2] went through my hand and then through my body. I know I'm going to die...'

'Éponine...' said Marius, looking at the poor girl sadly.

'Listen to me,' she said weakly, 'I have a letter for you in my pocket. I was asked to post it, but I didn't want you to get it. You see, I was a bit in love with you. Take your letter...'

She tried to smile at Marius but she closed her eyes for the last time.

Marius took the letter and read it:

> *4 June*
> *My dearest,*
> *We are leaving this house at once. Tonight we'll be at Rue de l'Homme-Armé, number 7, and in a week we'll be in England.*
> *Cosette*

Marius covered Cosette's letter with kisses.

'She still loves me,' he thought happily. 'But she's going away to England with her father. I can't join her. Nothing has changed. I don't want to live without Cosette.'

He took a piece of paper from a small notebook he carried in his pocket and wrote a letter to her:

2. **bullet :**

CHAPTER **EIGHT**

> *5 June*
>
> *Our marriage is impossible. I went to my grandfather and he didn't give his permission. I have no money. I hurried to see you, but you had already gone. You remember the promise I made you — I will keep it. I will die soon. I love you. When you read this my soul[3] will be near you.*
>
> *Marius*

He folded the letter, wrote Cosette's new address on the back and called a young boy.

'What's your name?' he asked the boy.

'Gavroche.'

'Very well, Gavroche, will you do something for me?' asked Marius kindly.

'Yes, of course.'

'Please take this letter to Miss Cosette on Rue de l'Homme-Armé, number 7.'

Gavroche took the letter and ran off into the night. When he got to Rue de l'Homme-Armé, he stopped in front of some doorsteps where a man was seated and asked, 'Is this number 7?'

'Yes, it is. Why?' replied the man.

'I have a letter for a girl who lives here.'

'I'm the girl's father; you can give it to me,' said Jean Valjean, taking the letter. 'Where does this letter come from?'

'It comes from the barricade in Rue de la Chanvrerie,' said Gavroche, 'and that's where I'm going now. Good night!'

---

3. **soul** : spirit of a person.

The barricade

Jean Valjean went back to his house and began reading the letter. He suddenly realized that Cosette had a secret boyfriend — Marius! This bothered Jean Valjean, because he loved Cosette more than his own life and he didn't want to lose her. When he read the words: *I will die soon. I love you. When you read this my soul will be near you*, he was suddenly happy.

'If I don't show this letter to Cosette, she'll never know what happened to this man and she'll never leave me,' he thought. 'She'll forget about him and we'll always be happy together, just me and Cosette.'

But in his heart he knew that he had no choice; he had to do *the right thing*. He had to think of Cosette's happiness and save the life of the man she loved.

Jean Valjean went to his room and decided to go to the barricades to fight. He opened a drawer where he kept his gun and put a handful of bullets in his pocket.

Then he stopped in front of a small mirror and looked at himself. Suddenly he started thinking about his troubled past. He remembered the terrible years at the Bagne of Toulon — nineteen years of unjust suffering. Then he thought of his meeting with the kind bishop of Digne who had given him new hope for the future. He remembered the town of Montreuil, where he had been mayor and owner of the glass factory. The image of poor Fantine came to his mind, too; he had kept his promise to her and had taken care of her daughter. But now there was one more thing to do.

'You're doing the right thing for Cosette,' he told himself.

Jean Valjean left his house on Rue Plumet and didn't know if he would ever return or if he would ever see Cosette again. He quickly made his way to the barricades.

The text and **beyond**

1 **Comprehension check**

Match the phrases in part A (1-10) with the correct phrases in part B (A-N) to make complete sentences. There are three phrases that you do not need.

Part A

1 ☐ During the revolt
2 ☐ Marius's friend Enjolras
3 ☐ Police inspector Javert
4 ☐ Éponine, who was wounded and then died,
5 ☐ Cosette wrote to Marius
6 ☐ Marius knew that he could not join Cosette
7 ☐ Young Gavroche took the letter to Rue de l'Homme Armé 7,
8 ☐ Jean Valjean discovered that Cosette had a secret boyfriend,
9 ☐ At first Jean Valjean didn't want to show the letter to Cosette,
10 ☐ Jean Valjean decided to go to the barricade

Part B

A and told him that she and her father were going to England.

B so he wrote her a letter and told her he couldn't marry her.

C and gave it to Jean Valjean, who was sitting on the doorstep.

D sent young Gavroche into the streets to see what was happening.

E when he read the letter that Gavroche had given him.

F the king and his family left Paris.

G but no one was home.

H many barricades were built in the Halles neighbourhood.

J gave Marius an important letter.

K but then he realized that he had to do the right thing.

L with his gun.

M was tied to one of the columns of the building.

N died during the revolt.

2 Writing

Write a brief description of these characters. Use the information from Chapter One to Chapter Eight to help you. There is an example at the beginning.

0 **Bishop:** *The Bishop of Digne was a kind old man who wanted to give everything he had to the poor. The people of the town loved him and the door of his home was always open for those who needed help. He greatly influenced Jean Valjean's character and future.*

1 **Jean Valjean (Mr Madeleine):** ....
....
....
....

2 **Fantine:** ....
....
....
....

3 **Mr Thénardier (Jondrette):** ....
....
....
....

4 **Javert:** ....
....
....
....

5 **Cosette:** ....
....
....
....

6 **Marius:** ....
....
....
....

7 **Éponine:** ....
....
....
....

CULTURE SPOT

Reading a painting

The famous painting, *Liberty leading the people* was created by the French artist **Eugène Delacroix** in 1830 in honor of the July Revolution of 1830. This revolution put an end to the reign of King Charles X of France. Eugène Delacroix was the leader of the Romantic school in French painting. While he was working on this painting, he wrote a letter to his brother saying, 'If I haven't fought for my country, at least I'll paint for her'. Liberty leading the people was first shown at the official Salon of 1831, an important art show in Paris. This splendid painting measures 260 cm by 325 cm and you can see it at the Louvre in Paris.

Look at the painting and answer the following questions.

1 What is the name of the woman leading the people?
2 What is she holding in her hands?
3 Describe the people in the painting.
4 Who does the young boy in the painting remind you of?
5 What can you see in the background on the right?
6 What is the general atmosphere of this painting?

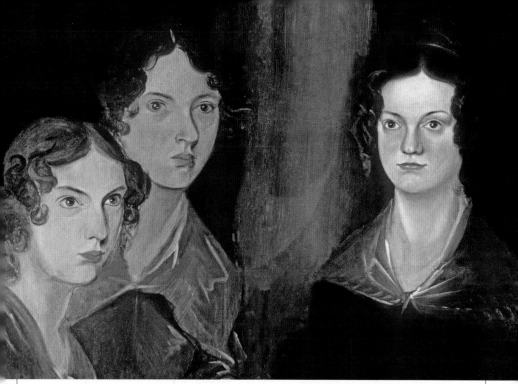

Portrait of Anne Brontë (1820-1849), Emily Brontë (1818-1848) and Charlotte Brontë (1816-1855), by Patrick Branwell Brontë (1817-1848), 1834, London, National Portrait Gallery.

Romantic heroes
in 19th century literature

At the end of the 18th and beginning of the 19th century in Britain, **Romantic poets and writers** became famous. They believed in the importance of individual feelings, the power of freedom, the beauty of language, nature, dreams and love.

Wordsworth, Coleridge, Byron, Shelley and Keats were five great Romantic poets from Britain, who wrote poetry which was different from that of the poets who lived before them.

During the 19th century, novels became the most popular form of literature. People from the middle classes had more time to enjoy

Mia Wasikowska and Michael Fassbender in the 2011 adaptation of *Jane Eyre*.

reading. Important writers like Jane Austen, Mary Shelley, and Charlotte and Emily Brontë began writing their masterpieces and creating Romantic heroes.

What is a Romantic hero? The Romantic hero is someone who has been rejected [1] by society and who lives in his/her own world, without considering the rules of society.

In *Les Misérables*, **Jean Valjean** is a great Romantic hero of French literature, and he can be compared to other Romantic heroes and heroines in British literature. In Charlotte Brontë's famous novel *Jane Eyre* (1847), Jane is the Romantic heroine: it is the story of a girl who had a sad and difficult childhood. When Jane grew up she became a governess [2] and fell in love with the man she worked for, **Mr Rochester**. However, he was already married to a mad wife who had to live in a secret room in his big home. When Jane found out about this she ran away, but could never forget the man she loved. In the end she went back to Mr Rochester, whose wife had died, and married him.

1. **rejected** : sent away, excluded.
2. **governess** : a woman who works for and lives with a family; she often educates their children.

Juliette Binoche and Ralph Fiennes as Cathy Earnshaw and Heathcliff
in Emily Brontë's *Wuthering Heights*, 1992.

In **Emily Brontë's** *Wuthering Heights* (1847) we meet another kind
of Romantic hero, Heathcliff. This novel tells the story of the love
between **Cathy Earnshaw** and **Heathcliff**. Their love story was
exciting and tormented[3] by social problems. Heathcliff was an orphan
who had grown up in Cathy's family, and he had no formal education
or position in society. When Cathy married another man, Heathcliff
could not accept her marriage. When Cathy died, he never forgot
her and began speaking to her ghost and doing other strange things.
Wuthering Heights is the story of a strong love that lasts even after
death. Although Heathcliff is not a kind or generous hero, he is still a
Romantic hero.

3. **tormented** : very difficult, troubled.

Boris Karloff as the monster in
Frankenstein, 1931.

In **Mary Shelley's** great novel *Frankenstein* (1818) the monster created by Victor Frankenstein became another Romantic hero. Everyone was afraid of the monster because of his huge size and ugliness. He desperately wanted to be part of society, but he was rejected by everyone, even by his creator, Victor Frankenstein. He became desperate and decided to take revenge on Victor Frankenstein's family. Romantic literature produced many heroes and heroines who are still popular today, and are often the protagonists of films and musicals.

1 Comprehension check

Answer the following questions.

1 What was the most popular kind of literature in the 19th century and why?
2 Why did Jane Eyre run away from Mr Rochester?
3 How did Heathcliff react to Cathy's death?
4 Why is the monster considered a Romantic hero in Mary Shelley's *Frankenstein*?

2 Discussion

Discuss with a partner.

1 Compare Jean Valjean with the Romantic heroes mentioned.
2 Can you think of other Romantic heroes or heroines?

Before you read

@Mp3 **1** **PRELIMINARY** Listening
Listen to the first part of Chapter Nine and choose the correct answer
— A, B or C.

1 Jean Valjean took Javert into a narrow alley
   A ☐ and let him go.
   B ☐ and shot him.
   C ☐ and fought with him.

2 Enjolras and the other rebels
   A ☐ won the battle.
   B ☐ left the barricade and went home.
   C ☐ died.

3 Jean Valjean wanted to save Marius
   A ☐ but it was impossible.
   B ☐ but the king's soldiers caught him.
   C ☐ and climbed down into the sewers with him.

4 Jean Valjean gave Thénardier thirty francs
   A ☐ and bought a gun.
   B ☐ and he unlocked the iron gate.
   C ☐ because Thénardier was poor and hungry.

5 Marius was wounded and was taken
   A ☐ to the hospital.
   B ☐ to the inn.
   C ☐ to his grandfather's house.

2 Reading pictures
Look at the picture on page 111 and answer the following questions.

1 Who do you see in the picture?
2 Where is this taking place?
3 What is the old man saying?

A new beginning

uring the night the terrible battle continued with gunfire and even cannons. The rebels fought bravely but they were losing the battle. When Jean Valjean arrived at the barricade Marius recognized him immediately.

'It's Mr Leblanc,' he thought; 'it's Cosette's father. He has come to fight with us!'

'Marius, do you know that man?' asked Enjolras, looking at Jean Valjean.

'Yes, I know him,' replied Marius, who was helping a wounded rebel.

Jean Valjean looked around and saw Javert, who was tied to a post in the inn.

A new beginning

Jean Valjean spoke to Enjolras, 'You're the leader, aren't you? Can I ask you a favour?'

'What do you want?' asked Enjolras impatiently.

'Let me kill this man,' said Jean Valjean.

'He's a spy... alright, kill him!' said Enjolras. 'I have other things to do.' He ran to his position on the barricade.

Jean Valjean untied the rope around Javert and pulled him out of the inn and into a narrow alley.

'You're free to go, Javert,' said Jean Valjean. Javert stared at him in amazement. Valjean continued, 'I don't think I'll leave this place alive, but if I do, you'll find me at Rue de l'Homme-Armé, number 7. *Now go!*'

'But why aren't you going to kill me?' Javert asked.

'Go!' replied Valjean. He shot his gun into the air, and Javert disappeared into a dark alley.

The battle continued and king's soldiers started climbing over the barricades. Soon all the rebels were dead, including Enjolras. A bullet hit Marius on the shoulder and he was in great pain; he fell to the ground. Jean Valjean's strong arms lifted Marius and put him on his shoulders.

'I must save him,' thought Jean Valjean, 'but how? There are soldiers everywhere.'

He looked around but he didn't know how to escape. Suddenly he saw an iron grill:[1] he went over to it and lifted it. With Marius on his shoulders, he climbed down into the darkness of the Paris sewers.[2] He could hardly see anything but he continued walking in the wet, smelly sewers. He knew that the sewers led to the river.

1. **iron grill :**

2. **sewer :** underground system that carries waste and rainwater away.

CHAPTER **NINE**

'Is Marius still alive?' Jean Valjean asked himself. 'I can't hear him breathing.' He put him down on a low wall and put his hand on Marius's heart — it was beating very slowly. 'Good, he's still alive!'

Then he put his hand in Marius's pocket and found a note which he had written.

My name is Marius Pontmercy. If I die, my body must be taken to the house of my grandfather, Mr Gillenormand, Rue des Filles-du-Calvaire, number 6, in the Marais neighbourhood.

He was ready to put Marius on his back when he noticed an iron gate. Outside the gate there was the River Seine. He shook it with both hands and tried to open it, but it was impossible. How could he possibly get out of the sewers?

Suddenly Jean Valjean felt a hand on his shoulder and turned around. He recognized Thénardier dressed in rags, but he did not give any sign that he recognized him. Fortunately, Thénardier did not recognize him.

'Do you want to get out of the sewers?' asked Thénardier.

'What do you mean?' asked Jean Valjean.

'You've killed a man,' said Thénardier, looking at Marius's body. 'Give me all the money you found in this man's pockets and I'll unlock the gate for you.'

Valjean quickly took all the money from his pocket and gave it to Thénardier, who opened the gate. Jean Valjean and Marius were finally out of the sewers and near the river.

Suddenly he saw a tall man in a long coat standing near him — it was Javert!

'What are you doing here, and who is that man' asked Javert, staring at Jean Valjean.

'Inspector Javert,' said Valjean quietly, 'please do me one favour. I promise not to escape. I have already given you my address so you know where to find me. Help me take this young man home. He's badly injured.'

Javert looked at Marius and shouted to his driver, who was waiting for him, 'Bring the carriage close to the river.'

Javert and Valjean put Marius in the carriage and they took him to Mr Gillenormand's house. One of the servants ran to call a doctor, and Javert and Valjean left immediately.

When Javert and Valjean were in the carriage again, Valjean said, 'Inspector Javert, another thing: let me go home for a minute. After that you can do whatever you want with me.'

'Very well,' said Javert, with a strange expression on his face. When they got to Valjean's house, Javert said, 'Go into your house. I'll wait for you here.'

Jean Valjean went into his house and climbed the stairs. Then he looked out of the window to see what Javert was doing, but the street was empty.

The next morning Javert's body was found in the river. He had ended his life by jumping into the river. He realized he had spent his life trying to imprison a man who was kind and generous, and now he could not live with himself any more.

As soon the doctor arrived at Mr Gillenormand's house, the old gentleman, whose eyes were filled with fear, asked, 'Doctor, please tell me the truth, will my grandson live?'

'I don't know,' the doctor replied. 'He's badly injured and has a high fever. It's difficult to say.' Mr Gillenormand spent his days

A new beginning

and nights sitting next to Marius's bed. Every day a white-haired man came to ask about Marius.

Four months later Marius was finally better and his grandfather was very happy. During all of this time Marius could think of only one thing: Cosette. One day he spoke to his grandfather and said, 'Grandfather, I want to get married.'

'Yes, of course!' said his grandfather, laughing. 'You'll marry your girl!'

'What!' cried Marius, who was beside himself with happiness. 'Are you serious?'

'Yes! I know that she's a lovely girl who loves you very much,' said Mr Gillenormand. 'Her father comes here every day and asks about you.'

Marius and his grandfather hugged each other and cried together.

The next day Cosette and Jean Valjean went to Mr Gillenormand's home. When Cosette saw Marius she was overcome with happiness, but she was afraid to show the world that she loved him.

Mr Gillenormand smiled at Jean Valjean and said, 'My grandson, Marius Pontmercy, wants to marry your daughter Cosette.'

Jean Valjean smiled and said, 'I agree!'

Mr Gillenormand looked at Marius and Cosette and said, 'You are free to love each other!'

The wedding took place two months later and it was a wonderful day for everyone. Cosette and Marius went to live in Mr Gillenormand's house, and although Jean Valjean was happy for the young couple he missed Cosette very much, and he went to visit her every day.

.

When Jean Valjean was home alone he thought about his past and it bothered him. 'What should I do? Should I tell Marius the truth about my past? No one knows the truth, not even Cosette.'

The next day he went to visit Marius.

'Marius, I have something to tell you,' said Jean Valjean, looking at Marius.

Marius listened quietly as Valjean told him everything about his past and his long years in prison.

'Why have you told me all this?' asked Marius, who was shocked.

'Because it was the right thing to do,' replied Valjean calmly. 'I can no longer live with a heavy heart; the truth is always the best thing, but please don't tell Cosette.'

Marius was very upset, but he didn't tell Cosette anything. He felt he couldn't trust Jean Valjean now and he asked him not to visit them any more. Jean Valjean was in despair and he became ill.

One day a stranger went to visit Marius; it was Thénardier, but Marius did not recognize him.

'I have a secret to sell you, Mr Pontmercy,' said Thénardier. 'Did you know that there's a thief in your family named Jean Valjean?'

'I already know this!' said Marius nervously. 'What do you want?'

'Ah, but you don't know this...' said Thénardier. 'During the revolt in June, I helped Valjean to escape from the Paris sewers. He was carrying the body of a man he had robbed and killed! He's also a murderer. This information will cost you money!'

'What!' cried Marius. 'The man Valjean was carrying was me! He saved my life and I didn't know it until now!' Marius ran towards Thénardier and pushed several thousand francs into his hand.

A new beginning

'You're a terrible man, a thief and a liar,' cried Marius. 'I should report you to the police straightaway, and the only reason I won't do that is because you saved my father's life at Waterloo! Now get out of here! I never want to see you again.'

As soon as Thénardier had left Marius went to find Cosette and told her everything.

'We must go to Valjean at once!' said Marius. 'We mustn't waste time.'

When they arrived at Valjean's house he was very ill, but happy to see them.

'Father, my dear father!' cried Cosette, hugging him.

'So you've forgiven me,' whispered Valjean.

'You saved my life!' said Marius, with tears in his eyes. 'Oh, I feel so ashamed of the way I've treated you.'

'Father, you must come and live with us,' said Cosette.

'No,' said Valjean, weakly, 'I'm going to die soon...'

'You must live, not die!' exclaimed Cosette.

'The time has come for me to tell you your mother's name. It was Fantine; she loved you so much and she suffered a lot,' said Valjean, lovingly. 'And now I must leave you, my dear children. Love one another always. Love is the most important thing in the world...'

He lay back his head and closed his eyes forever.

Cosette and Marius fell to their knees on either side of Valjean, and started crying silently. Valejan's head was turned to the sky and the light from the two silver candlesticks fell on his smiling, peaceful face.

The text and **beyond**

1 **PRELIMINARY** **Comprehension check**

**Read the summary of Chapter Nine and choose the correct answer —
A, B, C or D. The first is done for you.**

The revolt went (0) ....B.... all night. (1) .... the rebels fought
(2) .... they lost the battle. Marius (3) .... Jean Valjean as soon
as he got to the barricade. Jean Valjean saw Javert and asked Enjolras
if he could kill him. Enjolras gave him (4) .... and Jean Valjean took
Javert to a narrow alley, where he let him go.

(5) .... the night Marius was wounded by a bullet and fell to
the ground. Valjean wanted to save his life and carried him on his
shoulders. He climbed down (6) .... the dark sewers of Paris and
tried to find a way out. He (7) .... an iron gate near the River Seine,
but he couldn't open it. Suddenly Thénardier, (8) .... was dressed
in rags, said he could open the gate if Jean Valjean gave him all the
money he had found on the man's body.

Valjean gave him the money and got out of the sewers. On the river
bank he met Javert and convinced him to let him take Marius to his
grandfather's house.

Mr Gillenormand looked (9) .... his wounded grandson lovingly and
after four months Marius got better, and was able to marry Cosette.
Both Mr Gillenormand and Jean Valjean happily (10) .... to the
marriage.

After Valjean had told Marius the (11) .... about his troubled past,
Marius asked him not to visit his home anymore. Valjean was very
upset. Thanks to (12) .... Thénardier, Marius found out that Jean
Valjean had saved his life. So Marius and Cosette hurried to Valjean's
home and hugged him; but Valjean died shortly after.

0	**A** in	**B** on	**C** for	**D** at
1	**A** Because	**B** So	**C** Since	**D** Although
2	**A** bravely	**B** strongly	**C** brave	**D** hardly
3	**A** identification	**B** recognizing	**C** recognized	**D** knew
4	**A** permit	**B** permission	**C** permitting	**D** agreement

5	A	By	B	On	C	While	D	During
6	A	into	B	on	C	by	D	for
7	A	observed	B	looked	C	noticed	D	watched
8	A	who	B	that	C	whom	D	he
9	A	to	B	on	C	at	D	after
10	A	agreement	B	agreed	C	allowing	D	permitting
11	A	real	B	story	C	truth	D	true
12	A	greedy	B	greed	C	greedily	D	hungry

2 Hot seat

A chair in front of the class is the 'hot seat'. While you are sitting in this chair you are Jean Valjean, Javert, Fantine, Cosette or Marius.

A Questions for Jean Valjean

1 Did the Bishop of Digne's words and actions change you? If so, in what way?
2 Why did you help Fantine and then Cosette?
3 Were you afraid of Javert?
4 Why did you let Javert go free?
5 Why did you tell Marius the truth about your past?

B Questions for Javert

1 Why did you dislike Jean Valjean so much?
2 Had Jean Valjean become your obsession? If so, why?
3 Were you ever envious of Mr Madeleine?
4 Why did you jump into the river and end your life?

C Questions for Fantine

1 Did the Thénardier family make a good impression on you?
2 Did you ever suspect that the Thénardiers were dishonest people?

3   What was your job at the factory like?

4   How did you feel when you decided to sell your hair and your teeth?

5   Why did you trust Mr Madeleine?

D   **Questions for Cosette**

1   What was your life like with the Thénardier family?

2   How did you feel when the kind old man took you away from the Thénardiers?

3   Did you ever suspect that Jean Valjean had problems with the police?

4   Why did you fall in love with Marius?

5   What was married life like with Marius?

E   **Questions for Marius**

1   Were you ever able to fully forgive your grandfather?

2   Why did you fall in love with Cosette?

3   What did you write in the love letters to Cosette?

4   How did you feel about the revolt?

5   What are your feelings about Thénardier?

Now think of some more questions to ask each character.

3   Writing: an alternative plot

Choose a moment in the story where events might have developed differently. Describe what might have happened at this moment and summarize how the plot would have developed differently. Describe how this new plot that you have invented would finish.

CULTURE SPOT

Reading a painting

During Victor Hugo's life the Impressionist movement was born. **Pierre-August Renoir** (1841-1919) was a leading French painter of the Impressionist style of the 19th century. Impressionism was the first distinctly modern movement in painting that produced great French artists like Renoir, Claude Monet, Edgar Degas, Alfred Sisley and others.

Renoir was a very productive and dedicated artist. One of his most famous paintings is *Dance at Le Moulin de la Galette* (1876). In this important work Renoir shows an open-air scene of life in Paris during the late 1800s. Renoir was an acute observer of his time, and he enjoyed depicting the people and places of Paris.

This splendid painting measures 131 cm by 175 cm and you can see it at the Musée d'Orsay in Paris.

Look at the painting and answer the following questions.

1 Which are the dominant colours in this painting?

2 Who are the people and what are they doing?

3 How would you describe Parisian society at this moment?

4 What is the general atmosphere of this painting?

5 Describe the clothes that the men and women are wearing.

Les Misérables
The Movie

Title: Les Misérables
Year: 2012
Director: Tom Hooper
Starring: Hugh Jackman, Russell Crowe, Anne Hathaway

1 Look at the still and answer the questions.

A   Who are the two charcters in this still?

B   What part of the story does this still refer to?

C   Write your own caption.

2 Look at the still and answer the questions.

A   Where is Fantine and what is she doing?

B   Why are all the workers dressed alike?

C   How do you think the workers feel?

3 **Look at the still and answer the questions.**

    A What is Fantine going to do and why?

    B How does she feel at this moment?

    C Write your own caption.

4 **Look at the still and answer the questions.**

    A Who are the people at the barricades?

    B What are they shouting?

    C What chapter of the story does this still refer to?

5 **Look at the still and answer the questions.**

    A Describe Javert in this still.

    B How is he feeling at this moment?

    C Write your own caption.

6 **Look at the still and answer the questions.**

    A Who are the two protagonists in this still?

    B What are they celebrating?

    C What part of the story does this still refer to?

    D Write your own caption.

Les Misérables
The Musical

The award-winning, English-language version of *Les Misérables* was adapted from the French musical. It opened in London at the Barbican Centre on 8 October 1985 by the Royal Shakespeare Company. In 1987 this wonderful musical opened in New York City. It is one of the longest running musicals in history! It won eight Tony Awards and has been a great success ever since it opened.

1 Look at the still and answer the questions.

A Who are the protagonists of this scene?

B What do you think the red flag represents?

C What do you think the song they are singing is about?

2 **Look at the still and answer the questions.**

A Who are the two protagonists?
B What are they singing to each other?
C What part of the story does this still refer to?
D Write your own caption for this still.

3 **Look at the still and answer the questions.**

A What is happening in this still?
B Which protagonists can you identify?
C How are the protagonists feeling?

4 **Look at the still and answer the questions.**

A Do you recognize the flag on the stage of the theater?
B What is the audience doing?
C Write your own caption for this still.

5 **Look at the still and answer the questions.**

A What do you think these words mean, "Dream the dream"?

1 Picture summary

Look at the pictures and put them in the right order. Then write a short caption under each picture. Try to write in a sensational style, like the style of a popular newspaper.

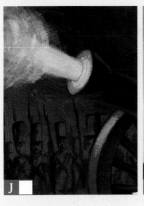
J

K

L

2 A graphic novel

Photocopy these pages, cut out the pictures and stick them on paper in the right order. Think of words to put in speech or thought bubbles to show what the characters are saying or thinking. Do not use the words that were used in this book! Then write at least one sentence under each picture to say what is happening.

3 Word square

Find the ten characters of the story in the word square and circle them.

S	C	O	W	A	T	C	H	T	H	F	R	I	É
F	N	T	S	O	M	J	A	V	E	R	T	E	P
O	O	E	H	R	C	E	A	M	E	A	O	I	O
H	X	P	I	P	È	S	R	A	T	S	R	N	N
B	A	J	E	A	N	V	A	L	J	E	A	N	I
I	R	T	B	R	H	A	I	D	C	V	E	T	N
S	C	L	E	P	F	B	R	M	B	A	A	H	E
H	K	Y	M	V	I	O	D	E	O	L	N	É	O
O	W	R	D	M	A	R	I	U	S	L	I	N	Z
P	A	A	F	A	N	T	I	N	E	P	U	A	S
F	Z	S	N	B	D	C	Y	O	R	E	X	R	D
C	N	M	F	R	A	D	H	O	A	E	J	D	S
F	A	U	C	H	E	L	E	V	E	N	T	I	O
C	A	S	F	G	A	V	R	O	C	H	E	E	S
C	O	S	E	T	T	E	P	O	L	R	X	R	O

4 Crossword: who was it?

Do you remember these characters? Read the clues and solve the puzzle!

Across

4 Thénardier's young son.

6 She had a doll called Catherine.

8 Javert wanted to put her in prison.

10 He spent 19 years in prison.

Down

1 He was a kind religious man.

2 He quarreled with his grandfather.

3 His body was found in the river.

4 He was the mayor of Montreuil.

5 She gave Marius an important letter.

7 He was the greedy innkeeper at Montfermeil.

9 He was killed during the revolt.

5 **Who said it?**

Look at the sentences below and match them with the person who said it.

1 ☐ 'Show me your passport.'
2 ☐ 'Of course he was telling you the truth.'
3 ☐ 'Can you look after my daughter for me, please?'
4 ☐ 'Please forgive me, Mr Madeleine, but I thought you were a man called Jean Valjean.'
5 ☐ 'Does she have enough clothes?'
6 ☐ 'This is a poor country and we have many expenses.'
7 ☐ 'It can't be Javert — I must be dreaming.'
8 ☐ 'You must, of course, dismiss me from my job because I don't deserve your trust.'
9 ☐ 'Cosette, take this bucket and fill it with water at the stream'
10 ☐ 'I'll have to ask the Mother Superior.'
11 ☐ 'These people are even poorer than me and they ask others for money.'
12 ☐ 'I have the address that you want.'
13 ☐ 'My father said that we have to leave for England.'
14 ☐ 'How can I possibly go to England?'
15 ☐ 'I will never give you my permission.'
16 ☐ 'I have a letter for a girl who lives here.'
17 ☐ 'She'll forget about him and we'll always be happy together, just me and Cosette.'
18 ☐ 'He saved my life and I didn't know it until now.'
19 ☐ 'Love is the most important thing in the world'

A	Javert	H	Fantine
B	Mr Thénardier	I	Marius
C	Jean Valjean	J	Mr Gillenormand
D	Gavroche	K	Cosette
E	Fauchelevent	L	Éponine
F	the innkeeper	M	the bishop
G	Mrs Thénardier		

This reader uses the **EXPANSIVE READING** approach, where the text becomes a springboard to improve language skills and to explore historical background, cultural connections and other topics suggested by the text. The new structures introduced in this step of our READING & TRAINING series are listed below. Naturally, structures from lower steps are included too. For a complete list of structures used over all the six steps, see *The Black Cat Guide to Graded Readers*, which is also downloadable at no cost from our website, blackcat-cideb.com.

The vocabulary used at each step is carefully checked against vocabulary lists used for internationally recognised examinations.

Step **Three B1.2**
All the structures used in the previous levels, plus the following:

Verb tenses
Present Perfect Simple: unfinished past with *for* or *since* (duration form)
Past Perfect Simple: narrative

Verb forms and patterns
Regular verbs and all irregular verbs in current English
Causative: *have / get* + object + past participle
Reported questions and orders with *ask* and *tell*

Modal verbs
Would: hypothesis
Would rather: preference
Should (present and future reference): moral obligation
Ought to (present and future reference): moral obligation
Used to: past habits and states

Types of clause
2nd Conditional: *if* + past, *would(n't)*
Zero, 1st and 2nd conditionals with unless
Non-defining relative clauses with *who* and *where*
Clauses of result: *so*; *so ... that*; *such ... that*
Clauses of concession: *although, though*

Other
Comparison: *(not) as / so ... as*; *(not) ... enough to*; *too ... to*